Breaking Free!

by Richard Flint, CSP

Copyright: 1999
Published: 1999
Revised Edition: 2001

ISBN# 0-937851-25-6

Printed in the United States of America. For information address Flint, Inc., 11835 Canon Blvd., Suite C-105 Newport News, VA 23606-2570 1-800-368-8255 www.richardflint.com

To Karen, my wife, and her family.
They have taught me about the true
meaning of life and its abundance.
For this, I am forever thankful.

Table of Contents

Chapter 1
THE STORY

The tragedy with most people is when they die
they leave behind a history lesson,
not a presence.

I don't watch a lot of television, but there are a few programs that I enjoy. One of my favorite channels is A&E. One of their programs that always captures my fancy is <u>Biography</u>. The line they use is that *every life has a story.* I have come to realize that more than a life having a story that *every life is a story.*

For years I heard it said that *inside of every person there is a book.* There is truth to that. But, every life is a book that begins with birth and continues until there is no one left who remembers they were present. That means death is really not an end if one has lived their life with presence.

Not long ago my very best friend, Fred King, died suddenly of a heart attack. Everyone talked about Fred being gone. Yet, Fred is not gone to me. His body may not be present, but he lives in my mind and his spirit is still part of my present.

Death can occur while you are still alive. Your life becomes a history lesson and not an ongoing biography. That means yesterday is all you have. When

1

you are trapped in the Circle of Sameness, you limit the presence you have. When all there is to talk about is yesterday, you cease to be a human who is continuing to write the next act. Your life becomes just a rerun and most people soon get tired of seeing the same old drama with the same old ending.

Have you noticed that when people become predictable, they become boring? Have you ever known a person who only had one story and they simply told it over and over? Did that get old? Did you find yourself not really wanting to be around them?

For you to have inner meaning you must be an ongoing series of essays drawn from the lessons that today is offering your life. When all you are is a history lesson, the personal book loses value because there is no continuation.

Every person is a story. Each day the story is being written through the behaviors they bring to the situations their life is facing. Each day that person must make a choice. They are either a repeat of yesterday or a new chapter being written. That choice creates the direction, the successes or the defeats of their life.

If you are simply a history lesson, your behavior will be designed to repeat, not improve. Therefore you won't see what is happening in your life. All your sight will be filtered through *what has been*, not *what is happening*. That means there is no present; there is only the past. Without the present, there is no connection point

2

to tomorrow. Your life becomes one dimensional — yesterday.

When you become locked in the Circle of Sameness, all your life is behind you. That means you are moving toward tomorrow while you are facing yesterday. This causes you to see where you have been and not what is in front of you. So, today becomes an instant replay of yesterday. Tomorrow is always frightening because it is an unplanned unknown. The creative center of your mind shuts down. When your mind finally understands you don't want to improve, it stops offering you the possibilities of improvement. It settles in to playing the reruns and it creates sight designed to stare at where you have been, not focus on where you are going.

Without the mind's creativeness, you soon give up on things getting any better. At that point you are no longer a person pushing for a better life. You now become a survivor who simply exists from day to day. You move from being a person who has a life to one who is merely existing and waiting to die.

In reality, you will die before you reach the casket. When you are no longer driven by a dream, you lose the ability to be excited by the events of life. When you are no longer desiring to improve, you find no meaning in today. Without that you must replay the tapes of yesterday to justify what is not happening in your life.

When you are no longer challenged by the unknown, you become a slave to your negative fears which keep you replaying the tapes of pain, disappointment and justification. The longer you play these tapes the greater control they have over your life.

I recently had a conversation with a young lady who is a living illustration of a life designed to repeat the tragedies that have made her an emotional prisoner for 42 years.

When she was 16 she met and married her husband. He was a man who knew how to manipulate all aspects of her life. His insecurities caused him to make sure she never reached a point where she could believe in herself. For 30 years he emotionally beat her into a mental state where she couldn't get beyond his control.

She divorced him, but he kept hanging around. His own insecurities wouldn't allow him to leave her alone. He would reappear and make her an emotional wreck.

Her lack of self worth kept letting him come back. In fact, she married him again and found herself exactly where she had left off in the divorce. He came back as a stronger person in her life. She had sent the message *I deserve the beatings you have given me.* So, what did he do? He increased the emotional beatings and mentally shattered her and physically pulled her down.

She divorced him again, but still allowed him to

hang around. There is no love, but he holds her hostage through the financial bindings he has on her. To face him and totally remove him from her life is something she feels she can't do. His years of emotional beatings have left her without any self worth. His financial bindings keeps a door open where he can come and go as he pleases. Each time he shows up he reestablishes his presence in her life by giving her another emotional beating.

Recently, she met someone who sees beyond the shell and who is interested in the person he knows she can be. BUT, she is torn. She loves the positive attention, but doesn't want her ex-husband to know she has anyone in her life. If he did, he might remove his financial support and leave her desperate.

So, what does she do? Does she walk away from what she has found that is offering her love and acceptance? Does she walk away from one who lifts her up, rather than knocking her down? Does she start making new tapes, or does she continue to replay the old tapes?

My bet is she will continue to play the old tapes. They are such a huge part of her personal belief system that she can't see beyond her pain of yesterday. What happens if she gives up the financial goodies the old relationship offers her and then this new relationship doesn't work? What happens if she totally closes the door to his financial manipulation and this new relationship goes away?

Her battle is between the fear of loss and the desire to have a life. My bet is the fear of loss will win. Her years of being a victim have left her too emotionally weak to take a risk. As much as she wants to close the door on yesterday and have this new life, she is a prisoner to the tapes that have killed her spirit. It is challenging for her *to understand that to create a better tomorrow you have to risk what you fear most.* The thought of total abandonment won't let her push her ex out and lock the door behind him. If she loses this battle, she becomes another member of the walking dead.

I wish she could see her life as more than a historical journal. I wish she could find the value in self acceptance and see the pain in self sabotage. I wish her desire for freedom was greater than her fear of loss. I wish she had the strength to race to the one who wants to hold her and tell the one who wants to destroy her to *get out of her life!* He has tortured her and is determined to keep her locked in pain.

She is a story. If she stays where she is she will simply be a tragedy without a happy ending. She will survive her time on earth and never really live.

Every person is a story! Who you are is based on what you believe about yourself. What you become is based on what tapes you choose to play. The future is not about the cards your life has been dealt; the future is about whether you are willing to risk shuffling the deck.

You are the result of what you believe about your

yesterday. The tapes you are viewing are the tapes you have made about the experiences of your life. What you believe about each event in your life is based on the tapes you play. What you will become is based on the tapes you use to define what today means to your life.

Life is a story you write each day with your behavior.

Each story has a different interpretation. If you view it from the pain, you get one edition. If you view it from the aspect of lessons learned to make you better, you get to view a different edition. *It is your choice as to what you see.*

I understand this on a personal level. My own journey has been designed by how I chose to view my yesterday. The greatest challenge my life has offered me is getting beyond yesterday. For many years I was a hostage to my yesterday. For many years I limited myself because of the tapes I chose to play. It has taken a great deal of effort and understanding to move beyond yesterday.

I am not telling you my yesterday never reappears. That "Old Me" is still living in a closet in my life. Every now and then an experience will happen that opens a small crack in the door and the "Old Me" peeks out. I am far enough along in my journey that I can recognize when it is happening and close the door. I don't take my growth for granted. I understand the need to consider yesterday as a reference library and not allow it to become the room I live in. When yesterday is your living room, you are a hostage to the negatives of yesterday. Freedom is not denying the fact of yesterday; freedom is the ability to use the experiences of life in a positive way.

Your choices about yesterday offer you a prison cell or freedom.

Most people who know me find it difficult to believe I could have ever been a prisoner in my own life, but I was. I lived as hostage to my emotional understandings about yesterday. My freedom began the day I decided there had to be more to life than a yesterday filled with pain. My freedom began when I realized I could control the tapes I was playing. Allow me to share my journey with you.

I was born in Marrerro, Louisiana. Marrerro is a suburb of New Orleans. There is not much I can tell you about my natural mother. Until I was 34, the only pieces of information I had were her name and that she was a prostitute in New Orleans.

There is nothing I can tell you about my natural father. On my birth certificate, the space for "Father's Name" has been left blank. I wish I could have known him. Even today, I find myself wondering about him. I wonder what he looked like, what type of personality he had and what part of my makeup did I get from him. There was a time when I would sit and sketch out what I thought he must have looked like. BUT, all of that is just my imagination playing.

I was adopted when I was two months old. The home I was adopted into was very unique. I can't remember my dad ever saying more than ten words at one time. My mother ruled our home. She was a very dominant person who had to have control of the home environment.

This created some interesting situations. My dad was silent and my mother was very vocal! When she said *jump*, you didn't ask *how high?* You just wondered *how long do I hang here!* The one thing you didn't do was ask my mother *why?* That led to instant punishment, and my mother was good at punishment. It was another of her control techniques. You soon learned to just *keep your mouth shut.*

My mother and I didn't have the best of relationships. Now, I was not a "bad" kid. I just asked a lot of questions and questioning my mother wasn't a smart thing to do. My mother saw any question as a threat to her authority, and she would be in control!

When I was twelve, my father walked in and informed us he had quit his job in the shipyards in New Orleans. We were moving to Oklahoma. By the middle of the following week we were in Lone Grove, Oklahoma taking care of a farm.

I remember the farm because it was one of the places in my life that taught me a work ethic. I had chores to do and was expected to get them done. That part was positive, but the increase in my mother's personal abuse was not. Each day it became more and more evident my mother didn't love me. As hard as I tried, I could not please her.

Two years later we moved into Ardmore, which was the major city in the area. My dad took a job as a mechanic with Cashman Truck Company.

When I was fifteen, my mother sat me down and informed me *if I was to live in the house I had to get a job and pay room and board.* Our family was not poor; we were a solid middle class family, but this was a calculated move by my mother. I now understand this was all part of a plan she had put into place.

So, each evening after school I would go to Luke's IGA Store and work until nine, then call my dad and he would come pick me up.

I had been sixteen for two weeks when my life experienced its first emotional earthquake. I had had many tremors, but never a major earthquake.

It was a Thursday evening, and I called my dad to come pick me up from work. My dad drove up in front of the store; I started walking toward the car when he opened the car door, stepped out and said, *Richard, wait a minute.*

Hey, when you are sixteen going on twelve, you don't always catch on quickly. BUT, when my dad stepped from behind the car, I began to see what was happening. My dad was carrying a suitcase. He walked over to me, sat the suitcase down beside me and said, *Son, your mother has decided you can no longer live at home.*

The pause that followed that statement was deafening. I remember watching his eyes and feeling pain from him and from me.

Fighting back the emotions that were filling his eyes, he reached out his hand, laid it on my shoulder and continued. *I'm sorry son. I don't agree with this, but I don't know what to do.*

At that moment I didn't understand what he was saying. I only knew what I was feeling. *How could he do this to me! I am not a bad kid.*

Years later I found out my mother had given my dad an ultimatum. *Either he goes or I leave you.* My dad was right; he didn't know what to do. He was in a corner and had to make a choice.

Squeezing my shoulder harder, he looked me in the eyes and said, *Don't you ever forget. I love you very much.*

As long as one feels loved, they can handle much of the trauma in their life.

I have never questioned whether my dad really loved me or not. I knew he loved me! It was that thought that had held me together for several years. As long as one feels loved, they can handle much of the trauma in their life. BUT, I will tell you without any reservation, my mother didn't love me. To her I was the enemy. To her I was a cancer she needed to remove. Day in and day out her behavior told me I was not wanted.

I have three sisters. We are all adopted, and each of my sisters had her own struggle with my mother. YET, I was the only one who was emotionally tortured. The emotional scars my mother inflicted on me can still trigger old tapes. As much as I understand about psychology, as many people as I have worked with, situations that remind me of my childhood can still trigger old tapes that emotionally turn me upside down.

That Thursday night my dad didn't walk back to the car — he ran! Opening the car door, he paused, looked at me and said with an emotional tremble, *You take care of yourself!* With that he got into the car and drove out of my life.

The next memory I have is of a man grabbing my neck and screaming at me *get out of the street!* I was standing in the middle of a four lane highway, tears streaming down my face as I watched my dad drive out of my life. My pain was unbelievable!

I have never known a more fearful time. I have never felt more alone. I had no idea what to do. I watched as my dad turned a corner, and as I stared down the dark street, I realized I had nowhere to go. I had just turned 16.

Put yourself in my shoes for a moment. What would you do? Where would you go?

I walked back to the suitcase, stared at it and finally told myself *you can't spend the rest of your life standing on a street corner.* I picked up the suitcase, walked into downtown Ardmore, went to the Hotel Ardmore and asked for a room. The look on the desk clerk's face was one of surprise, but I had cash so he gave me a key. I made my way up the stairs to the seventh floor, opened the door and without even bothering to turn on the light, dropped the suitcase, opened the window, crawled out onto the ledge, and sat there.

You can't begin to imagine the thoughts that were racing through my head:

- *How could my dad do this to me!*

- *I hate that woman!*

- *I should show them; I should jump; that would make them regret what they did.*

- *What am I going to do; I have no place to go.*

- *What did I do to deserve this; I am not a bad person.*

- *How could my dad love me and leave me.*
  How could he do that!

When I finally looked at my Timex watch, five hours had gone by. I crawled back into the room and told myself *if I jump, my mother will win! I won't give her that satisfaction.*

Every life has a wake up call. Most people just roll over and turn the alarm off!

Little did I realize that this was the beginning of a journey that was to take me through the rest of my life. Every life has a wake up call. The tragedy is that many people just roll over and turn the alarm off. That traps them in their Circle of Sameness.

The next morning I called Troy Howell. His daughter was my "girlfriend" and he was the only person I could think of who might help me. I explained to Troy what had happened. He told me to stay there. About twenty five minutes later he was in my room and for three hours we talked. Finally, he put the question in front of me that I was trying to avoid. *Richard, what are you going to do?*

I knew one thing for sure. I was not going back home. Troy helped me find a room with the lady who was the editor of the Daily Ardmorite. I paid her $5 a week to live in her house. She became the mother that I had never had. She would listen to me; she treated me like a person; she expected me to do certain things around her house. She praised me when I did them, and she reminded me when I didn't.

Each day I would get up, go to school, go to work, come home, and sit at the dining room table as long as I could. The last thing I wanted to do was go into that dark emotionally cold bedroom. You have no idea how many nights I would lic in bcd and cry myself to sleep. It was challenging to deal with the emotions I was going through.

Each day of high school challenged me. I couldn't go home to a family like my friends. Each day I would go back to my room and find myself learning to deal with both aloneness and loneliness.

When I graduated from high school, I wasn't sure what I was going to do. I had scholarships for college, but I wasn't sure. Again, Troy stepped in and helped guide me to my decision. He was right! I shouldn't stop now.

I really had it much easier in college than most. I was already adjusted to being away from home. This was nothing new. Still, there was this empty feeling. I couldn't get bcyond my yesterday. It did more than haunt me; it emotionally possessed me.

I wrestled with this scenario until I was a sophomore in college. The emotions would not go away. It affected everything I tried to do. I never felt people liked me; I was always waiting for the next person to hurt me. I withdrew into my own protective world and emotionally hid from people.

When you expect people to hurt you, they generally will!

My behavior made me an easy target for the negative people who will always find their way into your life. When you don't feel positive about yourself, you are always looking for your personal wrongs. AND, there are always people who will help you find them.

My life started to turn around with the appearance of Spencer Hayes in my life. During my freshman year, my closest friend was Johnny Bob. Johnny Bob was a "good old boy." He was one of those people who never saw wrong in anything. He was just an always "up" person. He always treated me like I really mattered and never found anything wrong with me. You know, when you expect people to hurt you, they generally will. But Johnny Bob gave me a safe feeling.

He came to me once and asked if I wanted to go with him to a meeting about a summer job. I didn't have anything to do, so off we went. The meeting was about working during the summer selling Bible books for the Southwestern Bible Company. I sat and listened as this man talked about the experience, the travel and the money. As I sat there one thought kept going through my mind — you could never do that!

At the end of the meeting as everyone was leaving a stranger walked over to me and asked if he could talk with me. I was startled, but said "okay." We must have talked for two hours and what he said to me made me angry and happy at the same time.

Richard, I don't know you, but I have a feeling you have had a rough life. You seem to be guided by your fears. I know what that is like. For years I lived as a prisoner to my past and controlled by the fears that went with that. You can't move forward until you get beyond that!

I had never had anyone nail me like that! I was angry that he knew that about me, but happy that maybe someone knew what I was going through.

I spent that summer selling Bible books door to door in south Alabama. It was one of the most frightening things I had ever done, but the turning point in my life. The trust Spencer had in me really helped me see beyond the tapes I had been programed with. Each week Spencer would call me to see how I was doing. The last thing I wanted to do was disappoint the one person who had expressed belief in me. That one thought kept me going when I wanted to give up. I kept telling myself *how would you explain that to Spencer.*

I not only made it through the ten weeks, but made enough money to pay for my education the next year. That summer started me believing in myself. Here I was a total stranger, living in a strange environment, knocking on the doors of people who didn't know me and they liked me! That experience made me question all the things my mother had told me about myself.

During my Sophomore year in college, I made the decision I had to confront my mom and dad. As much as I didn't want to, I knew I couldn't move forward with my life until I did.

I can remember the Saturday I got up and started the 62 mile trip to my mom and dad's house in Dickinson, Oklahoma. I must have given myself 100 reasons why this was not a good idea. BUT, the one reason for doing it was stronger than all the reasons I shouldn't do it. *I had to get by this in order to get on with my life!*

I got to my mom and dad's house, slowed down and drove right on by. My fear of facing them was so compelling at that moment there was no way I could stop. Sixteen miles down the road, I pulled off and had a conversation with myself. *If you don't do this now, you will never do it. How important is getting on with your life? If you don't finish this, you will become a permanent prisoner in your own life.*

I turned my car around and headed for their house.

When I got there, I parked in a service station lot and just stared at their front door. Finally, I took a deep breathe and drove into their yard.

I remember getting out of the car and running to the front door. I knew if I walked to the door, I would run back to my car. I got to the door and knocked. When the door opened, there stood my dad looking at me through the screen door. He froze and turned as white as a ghost.

Dad, it's me and I need to talk to you and mom.

Without even realizing what he was doing, my dad stepped right through the screen door and with one hug he told me all the emotions that had been pent up inside him. I have no idea what he was saying but he was just babbling on and on. He literally carried me into the living room still babbling.

Finally, he realized that my mother wasn't there. He paused and called for her to come out of the kitchen and see who was here. When my mother walked to the doorway between the kitchen and the living room, she just froze in her tracks. After a few seconds of getting her composure, she quickly untied her apron, and dropped in on the floor. Then she reached over and picked up her purse, took out her car keys, turned around, walked out the back door, got in her car and drove off. I never saw my mother again!

Now, do you think my childhood had an effect on my life? Do you think it presented me with challenges to work through?

Each of us is the product of where we have come from. We can choose to accept and go blindly forward, or we can take where we have been, learn from it and improve our today.

The tragedy I find with most people is they never complete their past, so they must constantly repeat the tapes they play. This means their beliefs, their behaviors are all defined by what they have never completed. That means each day is a repeat of the messages that have created a self destructive journey.

Each day I tell people *you don't have to be a hostage to your old tapes.* Each day I encourage people to *face where you have been and move beyond it.*

I watch the faces of people who have this desire to let go and move on. You can see it in their eyes. They know the need to get beyond their hostage situation, but the "Old Self" has had control for so long that the desire is quickly pushed down by the fear.

I will say it to you again. *The most powerful emotion in the human life is negative fear!* Once it gets a foot hold in your life, it is very challenging to ever get beyond.

So many times I have had people thank me, commit to taking their life forward, leave the safe seminar environment, go back to their old space, and slip right back into the "Old Behavior."

Each time their desire and resolve is held down

by their fear, they become less capable of ever moving beyond the tapes that have made today a repeat of the scripts of yesterday. What a tragedy to see someone give up on living and accept merely existing as the only journey.

The struggle to get beyond the tapes is not an easy one, but it is one that is possible. For many who have worked through it, it has been the single most challenging thing they have ever attempted, but also the most rewarding.

It is not something you can achieve overnight; it is not a journey that can be made on your timetable. It is a journey that will test every bit of the strength you have. The desire to free the "New You" has to be stronger than the fears the "Old You" will use to attack your life.

The process has four steps to it:

Step 1 • *Face what is really happening in your life.*

Step 2 • *Redesign the behaviors that have made it okay.*

Step 3 • *Strengthen the good things about you.*

Step 4 • *Reach out to others who are there to make you better.*

Notes

Chapter 2
UNDERSTANDING THE TAPES

*Life is a series of tapes stored in your mind,
but defined by your emotions.*

Several years ago people started coming to me at my programs and asking if I would consider working with them one on one. I found it interesting that they were willing to pay me to be their mental coach for a year. As I have worked in the lives of these people, I have learned some interesting things.

First, these are not people who are in denial about their life. They are not like the majority of people. My experience says most people don't want help. It is their painful life that gets them the attention they are looking for. They may ask for help, but then refuse the help when it is offered. The tragedy is that they could move beyond their pain, but choose to keep it as their pathway of living. Here they can complain about what life is not giving them and blame others for the pain they are experiencing.

These who come to me are talented, intelligent people who have reached a point in their life where they are tired of repeating their yesterday. They have strived to get beyond yesterday on their own, but have discovered they are trapped in the Circle of Sameness.

This Circle of Sameness is filled with behavior

designed to bring people back to the same emotional crossroads. It is an emotional journey that keeps you believing *I can never get beyond this.* To ensure this their emotional presence keeps playing the same negative tapes over and over. Each time the tapes are viewed, it destroys a little more hope. Each time the tapes are viewed, they walk away a little more drained and more convinced that *there is nothing I can do.*

You see, most people are designed to repeat, not improve. Each day they get up, enter their world and find themselves facing the same issues and same frustrations they have been facing. Each day their mind plays with what they would like to do, what they are not doing, what they should do — yet, at the end of the day they end up at the same place in their life.

Each day the lack of forward movement takes a little more of their creative energy. They find themselves giving in to things they know are not mentally and emotionally healthy for their life. They know, yet they find themselves justifying the Circle of Sameness.

Each day they find themselves losing some of their mental strength. They fight it, but because they are playing the same tapes, they generally lose the battle. Their "Old Behavior" has such a hold on their life. No matter how much they strive to break free and move forward, they are held hostage by the strength of the tapes their "Old Behavior" keeps playing.

Constantly, they find their negative emotions gaining a deeper hold on their life. They know what is happening, but because they are trapped in the Circle of Sameness they keep getting pulled back into the battle. Each time they get pulled back into the battle, they find themselves standing between the positive and the negative aspects of their life. Being trapped in the Circle of Sameness, heightens the battle. The New Person, who wants to break free, keeps getting knocked down by the "Old Behaviors" who have dominance in their life. That New Person is driven by the desire to improve; the "Old Behavior" is committed to keeping their life at the same pace and place it has been.

I believe that inside each person there is a "New You" that wants to push your life forward and see you achieve the success your talents will allow you to have. That "New You" is about making today better than yesterday. It is about using today as the launch pad for tomorrow. It is your imagination at full strength. It is your mind playing with possibilities and drawing pictures of where you want to be in your life. It is you focused on what needs to be done with today.

Your mind is never confused;
It is always clear on what needs
to be done!

25

The challenge comes with your emotional presence. The mind is never confused! The mind is always seeking solution and growth. It is always looking for the positive in everything in life. The challenge comes with the emotions that filter into your thinking. You see *all decisions pass through your emotions on their way to your brain.* That means if you bring the wrong emotions to an event, the emotions control what you are seeing. If your mind directs the journey, the picture is positive. If your negative emotions direct the journey, the picture will be negative.

Go back a minute to the statement *all decisions pass through your emotions on their way to your brain.* Imagine a multi-lane highway running between your emotional center and your brain. When you experience an event, there are two points it can enter. It can go in through your mind or enter through your emotions. Because most people are driven by their emotions, the entrance is the emotional highway.

The entrance to the highway is controlled by the most powerful emotion of life — FEAR! Of the four emotions that can hold a person hostage, this is the most powerful. When fear grips a human life, it can turn that life upside down and leave it lost in the jungle of "what if's."

Don't get me wrong, I am not saying all fear is bad. Each emotion has two sides — a positive and a negative. Your journey is directed by which aspect of the emotion you chose. Each path has a journey attached to it. That journey determines what an event will mean to your life.

Study this chart and see if it makes sense to you:

You will bring emotions to every event of your life. Those emotions will either strengthen or weaken your journey. The difference is on which side of an emotion you base the journey. Since most people are more emotional than they are logical, they enter on the left side. When you start the journey with worry, doubt or uncertainty, you fill the journey with the emotional family members who create skepticism, disbelief and procrastination. What does that do to the desire you started with? You're right! It drains the desire and gives your "Old Behavior" permission to play all the negative tapes from your past. In that design you can't win!

In that design you emotionally speed up. The faster you move emotionally the less mental strength you have. Your mind becomes silent as your emotions race forward with their presence.

The reality is that a positive emotion and a negative emotion cannot coexist. If you are being guided by negative emotions, you cannot see the positive that is happening. If you are guided by positive emotions, the negative cannot control your thinking.

The "New You" is about calmness, clarity and confidence. Yet, when the "Old You" is in control, the calmness is replaced with worry. What does that do to your mental strength?

The "New You" is about clarity, but when the "Old You" takes control, the clarity is replaced with doubts. What happens to you when doubts take over? What does that do to your mental understanding?

The "New You" is about confidence, but when the "Old You" takes control, the confidence is replaced with the feeling of uncertainty. What happens to you when you lose your confidence? How does that change your perception?

Whatever you do, don't underestimate the power of your "Old Behavior." It is one of the most formidable foes you will ever face. It knows you inside out. There are times when it will take a back seat and let you experience some feeling of success and then when you are starting to feel good about what is happening in your life, it will raise its ugly head, turn on an old tape and knock you down for the count.

How many times have you started forward only to be knocked down? How many times have you started and then been handed an emotional surprise that sidelined you? If I came and spent time in your life, how many things would I find that you have started, but never completed? Each of these unfinished events holds you hostage in the Circle of Sameness.

Each of these unfinished events is filled with negative emotions. These emotions keep sucking the positive energy from your life. Again, don't underestimate the power of the "Old You." It has been around your life for a long time; it knows your emotional hot buttons. To underestimate the power of the "Old You" to emotionally rule your life is to open yourself for emotional beatings.

Paul is a great example of a person living with a yesterday filled with unfinished events. I have known him for several years. He has been part of several of my audiences. Finally, one day he asked if we could talk. At breakfast he began to unfold this emotionally draining journey he had been on for several years. His life was one huge emotional slide. It seemed he had become a master at sabotaging his life. Listen to a few of the things he told me:

I seem to carry this anger around inside of me. At times I can't control it and it can turn my life upside down.

I have a few good days, but they don't last. Each time I start feeling good I look around until I can find something to take the good feelings away.

I don't like myself when I get in these depressed moods. I am no fun to be around and I know others don't enjoy having me there.

I wish I could control what is happening to me. I feel I am becoming more of this person I hate.

At that breakfast meeting Paul and I began to discuss the "Old You"/ "New You." We did something I do with most people like Paul that I work with — we gave his "Old Self" a name. We named him PooPoo. Now, does that sound strange? This "Old You" has to be recognizable. If you are serious about controlling the power "Old You" has over you, you must challenge him face-to-face. I had Paul talk to PooPoo out loud. A conversation in your head is not one you listen to. In fact, when that conversation is only in your head, you will emotionally talk yourself out of what you have agreed to do.

The conversations between Paul and PooPoo were designed to confront the control PooPoo had over Paul. When Paul talked out loud to PooPoo, he was having a conversation he listened to. He would challenge the thoughts PooPoo was feeding Paul; he would challenge the emotional upheavals PooPoo would throw at Paul. The more Paul confronted PooPoo the more aware he became of the tricks PooPoo would use. The more he confronted PooPoo the more he saw the power of PooPoo. The more he confronted PooPoo's emotional hold the more he was able to slow down and let the New Paul have some victories.

I could tell you stories about Joyce, Janet, Chris, Dale and more. All are people who were being beaten by the "Old Person" who emotionally ruled their life. It is so easy to give in to this Old Negative Behavior that is designed to hold you hostage in your own life.

This "Old Nature" doesn't want positive things to happen to your life. If and when they do, the "Old Nature" will work to find the negative. The easiest way is to turn on those old tapes. You know — *the ones you keep playing over and over that remind you of the pain and failures in your life.*

This "Old You" doesn't want you to grow. It knows the more you understand its tricks the more you will know about controlling its presence in your life. So, it is constantly working to steal your focus, make you procrastinate, listen to the negative. It wants you to sit down and relive the past. Why? Because the past is about the negative, not the positive. Yes, the past has positives, but most people don't play those tapes. The tapes they play deal with the pain, the hurts, the negatives their journey has taken them through. By playing these tapes the "Old You" can hold you hostage in this Circle of Sameness. Once you believe *this is the way it is going to be*, you start designing a journey to repeat, not improve.

Once you become locked into repeating, rather than improving, you are a prisoner to the emotional beatings you keep inflicting on yourself. Think about it for a moment. How many times do you beat yourself up? How many times do you talk yourself out of enjoying the good that is happening in your life? How do you do that? You start listening to the negative tapes you have been listening to for years. Each time you turn those tapes on you get sucked right back into behavior designed to take you around another lap in the Circle of Sameness. Each lap strengthens the "Old You" and weakens the "New You." Each lap strengthens the message *I can't get out of this.* Each lap steals a little of your desire, adds another layer of doubt on top of your dream and brings a greater sense of reality to the negative tapes. Do this long enough and inwardly, you give up.

This giving up is not failure; this giving up is human defeat. Failure is just an option that didn't work. So, you look at the next option, calm yourself and move forward.

Defeat is the acceptance of the negative as the way it is.

Defeat is the acceptance of the negative as the way it is. At this point you stop looking for the exit; at this point you give in to staying the same; at this point there is no turning the negative tapes off. They are the only emotional movie you are watching. At this point you become another member of the walking dead.

The human spirit is not about giving up; it is about continuing to push forward. When the human spirit dies, so does the dream. Without that dream there is no direction and the only thing you can do is live in the Circle of Sameness.

The human spirit is not about giving up, it is about reaching for the next mountain. When that spirit dies, you will see the mountain, but be controlled by the fear of climbing it. Therefore, life becomes *what you should or might do someday.* At this point life becomes a series of disappointments you keep justifying.

The human spirit is not about giving up; it is about personal improvement. When the human spirit gives in to the "Old You," sameness becomes the mission. At this point you start looking for the reasons; you accept the negatives without challenging them; you stop listening to those who want to help you and only listen to those who help you validate your story. At this point you start criticizing those who are improving and refuse to see the good in their life. All of these behaviors are designed to prove *this is what my life was meant to be.* Each time I hear that statement I know I have met a person who has given up on the "New You" and given in to the "Old You."

Each time I hear a person put their self down I know I have met a person who is justifying the negative tapes they are playing. They are refusing to look beyond yesterday; they are refusing to see anything except the wrongs and injustices in their life.

If you strive to show this person the exit out of the Circle of Sameness, you become the enemy. Your positive presence can bring out the worst from the "Old Self." They will emotionally attack you; they will find fault with all you say; they will mock you; they will dismiss what you are saying as *just more hype and that stuff is for the weak.*

These lives are about yesterday! Rather than being a reference center filled with volumes of experiences both good and bad, yesterday becomes their living room where they sit and replay all the negative tapes they have made.

As long as a person continues replaying the wrongs of life, they will keep designing behaviors to repeat them. Each time they repeat a behavior it strengthens itself as a belief.

As long as a person continues replaying the pains of yesterday, they keep designing experiences to repeat the pain. They will keep going back to situations that feed the pain. Each time they do this they strengthen the pain and weaken their ability to move beyond it.

Study what one feels about their yesterday and you will know their expectations for tomorrow.

Repeating is about replaying old tapes. It is about getting lost in what was. That means feasting on the negatives until they own your emotional understandings about what you experienced. If you study what a person feels about their yesterday, you will know their expectations about tomorrow. The feelings you bring from past experiences create the understandings you have for today. As long as those feelings are negative, you will create tapes that replay the wrongs. Only when you find the positive lessons in the event, can you move beyond it.

Repeating is about looking backwards; it is about not having a plan for today. When you repeat the journey you have already made, you are not searching for the next part of the growth plan. Many people would tell you they do that because they enjoyed where they had been. In reality, repeating is easier than facing the fears that keep them from completing the journey they started.

The "Old You" is a master at using guilt, anger and fear to lock you in the Circle of Sameness. These three are the gate keepers who constantly push you back when you get close to breaking out. They stand there as the great intimidators whose presence is made stronger each time they can shove you back into the wrongs and pain of yesterday. Study your life. Notice how many times you have gotten serious about breaking out of the Circle of Sameness only to have guilt, anger or fear push you backward. Notice the tapes the "Old You" turns on to wear your desire down and take away that spark of desire that says *I want out of this lifestyle.*

Breaking free of the Circle of Sameness is not about defeating the "Old You." It is about designing an environment where the "New You" has a greater presence than the "Old You."

The "Old You" wants you to go to war. It knows you don't have the battle plan to overthrow its powerful presence in your life. When you go to war against the "Old You," you make it the emphasis. Without realizing it, you are feeding its behavioral presence.

The way to defeat the "Old You" is to place the emphasis on the "New You" that is filled with the positive desire that gives your life happiness, personal fulfillment and freedom. To achieve this your emphasis must be on the "New You" and not the "Old You."

Does that make sense? You don't overcome the

"Old You" by fighting the negative. You overcome the "Old You" by finding the positive. Each time you go after the negative, you turn the negative tapes on. This feeds the "Old Behavior" and gives it a more visible presence. Doing this will only strengthen the "Old Behavior."

Placing the emphasis on the "New You" means making new tapes. This is feeding your desire, not your guilt, anger and fear. This is not avoiding the negative tapes; it is controlling their power in your life. Let your mind design the positive, rather than your emotions feed the negative. This allows you to edit the old tapes by making the opportunity more important than the obstacle. This allows you to see what is ahead, rather than hiding in the past. This will feed your desire, rather than let your emotions feast on the negative.

What we are talking about is a change of energy flow in your life. We are talking about giving your mind more control than your emotions.

Notes

Chapter 3
THE CHALLENGES

One of the great challenges people face is being able to find the lessons that yesterday offers, rather than the pain they keep staring at.

There is no way of getting around the fact that my childhood had an effect upon my growing up. What many don't understand is that the tapes you make as an adult you can edit. The tapes you make as an child are permanent memories. As much as you strive to get around them, at any second an event can open an emotional door that triggers a flashback.

More than once this has happened to me. When I was 32 years old I needed a passport. Now understand, I had never seen my birth certificate. When my dad died, I had searched all through his papers trying to find it, but to no avail. So, I wrote the Department of Vital Statistics and requested a copy of a birth certificate for Richard Lee Flint born February 3, 1945. I received a reply informing me I had never been born. I raced to the mirror, looked at the person in the mirror and knew there was something wrong here.

My other thought was *if I could get a certified copy of the fact I had never been born, I could get all the income tax money back I had paid in.* After all, if I wasn't real, why should I pay taxes!

I called my sister Rita, who is two years older than me, and explained what was happening. She had found a letter from my birth mother in my dad's personal papers. Armed with the knowledge of her last name (Swain), I flew to New Orleans, went to the Department of Vital Statistics and again asked them to check for a birth certificate for Richard Lee Flint, born February 3, 1945. The lady came back and informed me there was no record of my birth. I then asked her to check for Richard Lee Swain, born February 3, 1945. Sure enough, there it was.

I don't know if you can understand the feelings that went through me. Not only did my mother not want me, but she never legally adopted me. I think there was a message in her actions. For the next several months I went through the legal process of having my name changed to Richard Lee Flint. Each time I had to face a part of this legal issue, I could see my mother looking down and smiling that smile that always said *I won!*

As much as you will strive to get beyond the tapes from your childhood, there will always be situations that will trigger emotional memories that will open mental files that will flip on an old tape. Each time the tape plays it will pull you back to an emotional situation you have been through.

A challenge is a situation you have faced and moved beyond; a problem is a situation you have run from.

Every event is viewed as either a challenge or a problem. The difference is the emotions you have brought to each. A problem is a situation you have never completed. Without the completion it remains an open file in your mind. Each time the tape is switched on you have to deal with all the emotions that situation has brought to your life. For most this is a real time of struggle. The emotions they are feeling create negative pathways. Each negative pathway takes them into a room of memories that keep replaying all the wrongs, all the hurts and all the pain.

A challenge is a different pathway. A challenge is a situation you have faced and moved beyond. That doesn't mean it will never come back again. BUT, when it reappears, you have been there and faced it. The lesson has been learned, and it can't emotionally hold you hostage in a room filled with negative emotions.

Yes, for years I struggled with problems. I was great at replaying all the old tapes. The Old Richard was in total control of my life. Each time I turned around I found myself staring at something my mother had said about me. It was only when I made the journey to my parents house that I began the process of reprogramming the tapes my mother had handed me.

Time and time again as I have worked with people, I have had to show them the necessity of going back and completing an event. They had to do this to move forward, rather than exist in an emotional Circle of Sameness.

Most people really don't understand the power of the "Old Them." That inner emotional person is a negative intruder in their life. Each time they try to move forward, that "Old Negative Person" raises its head and flips on an old tape that can emotionally flatten them. Each time they seek to find the lesson, that "Old Negative Person" clouds their positive quest with old tapes of doubt, worry and skepticism.

Only when they are strong enough to stand strong against the "Old Negative Person" can they ever move beyond the emotional hold it has on their life.

The most common question I am asked is how *does the "Old Negative Person" assert itself?* The attack is done through some very powerful emotions.

One of these is GUILT! Guilt is a hostage taker. It is an emotion that makes you question any decision you have made. It is an emotion that makes you feel sorry for the person who has created your pain. It is an emotion that makes you give in to allowing another to take control of your presence. You can know what is right, but come face to face with guilt and do that which will cause you to repeat the painful event, rather than move beyond it.

For so many years I lived with guilt flooding my life. I can't tell you I loved my mother. For years that created a tremendous amount of guilt for me. My biblical upbringing was filled with teachings about loving everyone, even those who caused you pain. I found myself constantly in a wrestling match between what I was feeling and what I was hearing.

My guilt was handled the day I realized that love has several layers to it. Love is not about always agreeing with what one says or does. Love is about seeking to understand the person. For love is about slowing down and finding meaning, rather than racing forward and not facing the issue. Love is not about blindness; it is about an inner light that allows you to see beyond your limited perception.

Love begins with concern. I can say *I was concerned about my mother.* It was that concern for her and my dad that caused me to make the journey home. I wanted to complete the conversation I never had with my mother. There were things I needed to say to her. These feelings had haunted my life for years. I needed to have this conversation to get on with my life. When she refused to face me, my part had been completed. When she walked out the back door, no longer could she hold me an emotional hostage. I had opened the front door of my life to gathering understanding; her walking out the back door and driving off told me I was not the real issue. With that understanding my guilt could be handled.

You have to understand how another person can use guilt on you. They are in control of the script. They never let you participate in writing the story. They know you well enough to throw the emotional issues at you that make you feel bad about yourself. When you no longer feel bad about yourself, they can no longer manipulate you with guilt! *The freedom from guilt is when you take over the writing of your story.* When you are writing the story, you control what tapes are being played. When another person can emotionally manipulate you, they control what you are listening to and seeing. Take that away from them and the guilt can no longer hold you as their emotional slave.

Not long ago I agreed to work with a very special couple through my Private Coaching Program — Ted and Nancy. What super people!

My challenge in Ted's life was to get him focused on the journey to business freedom. As successful as he is in his business, there is something missing. The realization we came to was this was a script he was handed. Even though it fit his talents, it was not what he really wanted for his life. For years he has searched, but each time the old tapes sucked him back into a script someone had written and he had accepted. It is exciting to tell you he is taking control of his life. He is slowly marching toward happiness, personal fulfillment and freedom.

My challenge with Nancy was getting her to meet Nancy. She is a beautiful woman who has been lost in the shadows. Nancy's issue was getting beyond the guilt her mother had flooded her life with.

Nancy's mother was a master manipulator. She knew how to emotionally get inside Nancy and make her feel guilty. She would make her feel like she wasn't a good daughter. Now, most daughters want their mother to be proud of them. Nancy's mother knew the right things to say to make her feel like she had let her mother down. The result was a lady filled with guilt and being held an emotional hostage by a manipulating mother.

Month after month we would talk about Nancy confronting her mother's behavior. That was not a conversation Nancy wanted to have in the beginning. How could she do that! We were talking about her mother. To talk back to her mother was to be disrespectful. To talk back to your mother is a sin!

Nancy had to face the fact that her mother would always be her biological mother, but that her behavior said *she really didn't respect Nancy as a person.* Nancy was her emotional slave. If she did not "jump" when Mom said "jump," there was hell to be paid.

Finally, Nancy reached a point in her growth journey where she could admit that her mother was really a negative influence in her life. If she was to move forward, she had to confront her mother's behavior. She could not have that conversation as a child talking to its mother. That conversation had to be an adult talking to an adult.

I was so proud of the New Nancy. The confrontation took place and the New Nancy didn't back down. Her mom used every technique she knew but this time it didn't work. Nancy walked out feeling free from the guilt and able to move forward with her life. Granted, her mother will still test the water, but once Nancy proved she could move beyond the point of being her mother's emotional hostage, she has not gone back.

The second powerful emotion that is used is BLAME. Many don't understand the power blame can hold over a human life. It is very challenging to stand strong within yourself when you accept the blame that another dumps on you. Can you see how blame and guilt work together?

My mother was a person who never physically felt well. Any time there was conflict she couldn't control, she would get sick. Her physical ailments were the shotgun she used to spread blame.

I can remember some of her favorite statements:

• *See what you have done. You have made my heart speed up. I am going to have to lie down. I can't believe you would do that.*

• *Now see what you have done. You have made my blood pressure go up. I need to take some medicine and lie down.*

• *Why do you have to ask so many questions? You are making my migraine come back. Just look at what you have done.*

Blame really is an interesting emotion. Blame takes the emphasis off what is happening and forces one to believe they are the reason for the bad that is happening. Blame is designed to make sure what one doesn't want to talk about doesn't get finished! So many conversations filled with good intentions get derailed through the use of blame.

When Wanda entered my life, she was a shell of a person. As a child, she had a mom who used blame to make her feel guilty. All through her childhood and her young adult years, she believed she was the reason everything bad happened. When she got away, she married her mother in a male body. Her husband was a negative person who always moved from one crisis to another. Rather than being responsible for his own life, he would always blame Wanda for the wrongs. Having grown up in the same environment, she would just accept the emotional beatings. After all, that was the script she had been programmed to live with.

When she appeared in my life, I talked very openly to her about what the journey to her personal freedom would involve. It meant she would have to confront her mother and her husband — in that order. My question was simple: *can you handle this?* Her response was *yes!* Having seen this struggle before, I knew it would take months before she would be able to face just one of these issues. The first step was getting Wanda to believe in Wanda. She needed to have some successes that neither her mother nor her husband could take away from her. She needed a period of time where Wanda felt good about Wanda. She needed to throw some success parties where she was the only guest.

After seven months of finding positives to celebrate and throwing private parties we didn't tell her husband about, she was ready for the first step. That step was going home and facing her mother. It meant not taking responsibility for the wrongs her mother would throw at her. It meant holding her mother accountable for her behavior. The first trip home didn't turn out too well. As strong as Wanda had become, she was not strong enough to face her mother who had years of practice at using blame on her.

Wanda came back feeling she would never be able to get beyond this. She still felt it was wrong to have these types of conversations with her mother. After all, we were talking about her mother. To confront her mother with this stuff was disrespectful.

As I listened to all this, I knew her mother had won this round. Wanda had been knocked down, but she was not out!

Again, the need was to understand her mother would always be her biological mother, but that her behavior said she didn't respect Wanda as her daughter. If Wanda really wanted her mother's respect, she would have to force the redesigning of their relationship. The downside could be her mother never wanting to see her again. We practiced that conversation over and over. Wanda had to understand this was a real possibility, and she had to be okay with that result.

Isn't it amazing how one can be trapped in a prison of pain and still fight to stay there? Blame and Guilt are such powerful hostage takers.

Several months later when Wanda made the trip back home, she was prepared. She told her mother that she loved her, but didn't appreciate how she treated her. As her mother would throw blame and guilt at her, she would refuse to be the victim. *She kept turning the conversation to the behavior of her mother, not her.* The stronger Wanda's presence became the more her mother backed down. By the end of the weekend Wanda had shown her mother that she would no longer be treated like an emotional toy her mother could play with.

Armed with this new belief in herself, she was ready to face her husband. In reality he would prove to be a tougher challenge than her mother. He knew her love and concern for their two children and was a master at using them as his focal point for guilt and blame. I have never met a mother who couldn't be manipulated by the pain her children were going through.

At this time each child was having its own personal struggle. As Wanda would approach her husband with an issue, he would turn around and blame her for the struggles the children were having. BUT, the New Wanda was prepared. Each time he would throw blame and guilt, she would come back with accountability and responsibility. She wouldn't be derailed by his tactics. She stayed focused and pushed the conversation forward, rather than allowing it to become another old tape.

Today, Wanda has a great relationship with her mom. They are mother and daughter; they have fun together.

However, Wanda's husband is gone. He presented Wanda with an ultimatum. When she called his bluff, his ego couldn't handle the result. Today he is a lonely man looking for his next victim. It isn't Wanda!

The third powerful emotion the "Old You" uses to hold you an emotional hostage is FEAR! This is by far the most powerful of these emotions.

Fear is the parent of all emotions. I have taught for years that 99% of all decisions you want to make never get made because of negative fear.

It is important you see what you just read! I qualified the type of fear I am talking about with the word "negative." Not all fear is bad. There is positive and negative fear.

Positive fear is energy that slows you down and allows you to ask the right questions. In asking the right questions you create an environment of calmness, clarity and confidence. This positive fear is driven through the mind taking control and seeking a solution to what it is facing.

Negative fear is energy that speeds you up and creates an environment filled with doubts, worry and uncertainties. Each of these is designed to shut your mind off and only see through your emotions.

Your mind is never negative; it is your positive partner who is always seeking the solution.

I believe your mind is never negative. I believe your mind is your positive partner who, when given permission, will always take you toward solution. It is your positive partner who always sees what is best for your life. It is your growth partner who is always focused on what behavior will take you through this part of your life journey.

The challenge most people face is that they choose to live through their emotions. Events enter their life through their emotions and are filtered and defined before they reach the mind. By the time a situation travels the emotional pathway to the mind it is filled with doubts, worry and uncertainties. Because your emotions have designed the pathway, your mind doesn't get to show you the positives. Even when it tries, you are so emotionally drained you can't see it. An emotionally exhausted person isn't willing to listen to what their mind is trying to tell them. They are so drained, they just see it as more work they don't have the energy to implement.

To really experience growth you must be aware of the informational entry point in your life — mental or emotional. The entrance point designs the journey the information will take. All information enters, gets processed, defined and given back in some form. The processing creates the meaning. If information is processed through negative emotional filters, the result is negative feelings which cloud your ability to see the positive. Therefore, life's situations become a negative journey. The result is a life that becomes an emotional hostage.

If the information enters through your mind and gets filtered through your calmness, clarity and confidence it creates a different vision you are to use for your journey. The journey now becomes a positive experience which fills the life with experiences of growth and freedom.

For instance:

I believe the difference between *a problem* and *a challenge* is the entrance point into your life.

The difference between *an obstacle* and *an opportunity* is simply the entrance point into your life.

The difference between *a difficulty* and *a solution* is simply the entrance point into your life.

Anything that is defined by negative fear will lack creative understanding. Anything that is controlled by the family members of negative fear will be lost in the maze that pushes you away from solution and toward doubtful worry. Please don't ever forget:

A positive emotion and a negative emotion cannot coexist!

One of the two will be in control, and the controller creates the pathway you are traveling. When an event enters through your emotions, the majority of the filtering will be done through the negative. That will keep your mind from referencing the positive connection points.

When the event enters through your mind, the filtering is done through positive connection points. This keeps your emotions from controlling the event with negative emotional tapes.

In my working with human behavior I have found there are five negative fears that constantly hold people hostage. See how many of these you have seen at work in your life or the life of someone you have known.

The Fear of Abandonment:

If I do what I know I need to do, I might be left alone!

For many the fear of having to face life alone is more than they can handle. They would rather have someone in their life who mentally and emotionally and yes, sometimes physically abuses them, than face life alone.

Sally put it this way: *I know I would be better off without him, but then I wouldn't have anyone in my life. Having him is better than having no one in my life.*

This comes with a powerful negative tape, laced with fear and designed to not allow a person to find value in themselves. This life is a prime candidate to be held hostage by guilt and blame.

The Fear of Rejection:

If I do what I know I need to do, someone may not like me.

For many the need to be liked is so important they will do anything in order to have others in their life. Acceptance is everything to them.

Peter put it this way: *Hey, I'll admit it. I need people in my life. I need them to like me. If that means playing their game, then that is what I will do.*

Martha said it this way: *I don't have much self esteem and I know it. I need people to like me. I will do and be what they want me to be if it means they will like me.*

Peer pressure doesn't end in adulthood. In fact for many it gets worse. Rejection is an interesting study. It is not about another liking or not liking a person. It is about a person liking their self. I really believe that no one rejects another person. Rejection is one's own feeling about self being translated into their behavior. It is your behavior saying to others what you feel about yourself. Can you see where one who needs to be liked by others is an easy target for guilt and blame?

The Fear of Failure:

If I do what I know I need to do, it may expose the fact I can't do it.

Too many people have been raised with the wrong understanding of failure. They have had failure programed into their life as a negative. They see failing as a sign of weakness.

They have had their failures used as weapons of disappointment against them. It has been used to create self doubt; it has been used to create the feeling of unworthiness. Each of these creates the wrong mental picture of failure.

There are actually three words that have to be linked together to see the total picture — success, failure and defeat.

<u>Success</u>: *my judgments and feelings concerning the events of my life.*
<u>Failure</u>: *my judgments and feelings concerning the events of my life.*

The difference between these two is simply perception. That perception is created by the tapes one brings to the event they are facing. When a person sees failure as only part of the bridge of understanding, it changes their entire thought process. True success is understood when a person can see failure as simply an option that didn't work. It is not an end all; it is not a point of disgrace; it is not a permanent "F" tattooed on their forehead for everyone to see. It is simply one event on the success journey designed to teach you a lesson. That lesson can only be seen when you slow down, face the event and open yourself to learning, rather than closing yourself to self discovery because of the fear of failing.

Tie this fear back to the other two negative fears. *If I fail, others will think less of me and I may find myself without anyone in my life.* If a person slips into that thinking process, they will see failure as a means of personal disgrace. The result will be that they walk away from anything that seems too tough. What happens is they start several things, then the fear of failure takes over and they walk away by making excuses or having a reason why *this is not a good time for this in their life.*

This leaves their life with several incomplete events. Each of these feeds their negative side.

If and when that happens, they bring the third word into their journey — defeat. Defeat is *walking away from an event before the lesson has been learned.*

I view success, failure and defeat as a bridge. On the right side is the pathway to success. On the left side is the pathway to defeat. The bridge is failure. Every event finds you standing on the bridge. Every event your life is handed will contain moments of doubt, worry and times of uncertainties. These are the moments when you have to choose which direction you will turn. If you face success, you will see the lesson, make the decision to move forward and find the journey to self improvement.

If you choose to move toward defeat, you will be consumed by the fear, and find an excuse to avoid learning from this event. Then, the next time you face the same event (and it will keep reappearing), you will find it difficult to see anything other than your negative fears. That will strengthen the defeat and weaken you as a person. The result is the Circle of Sameness which will just take more and more energy from your life. This Circle of Sameness is designed to make you an emotional hostage in your own life.

Negative fear will turn opportunities into obstacles, challenges into problems, improvement into change and leave you with a dark feeling that *this is what my life was meant to be.* The greatest tragedy about this is you give up on life! When you give up on life, you start merely existing.

Existing is mental death that lets you see life only through your emotional presence. At this point the "Old Negative You" has total control. Every now and then you will feel this inner urge to break free, but the "Old You" has such a powerful grip on your life, it will give you scarcely a moment to sense maybe you can break out. Then, it will raise its powerful presence and turn on the old tapes that are based on guilt, blame and fear. These emotions will steal the desire and leave you with an even stronger feeling that says *my life will never get any better.*

The Fear of Loss:

If I do what I know I need to do, it may cost me more mentally and emotionally than I am willing to pay to have it.

One thing that my working with human behavior has taught me is *most lives don't fall apart at the level of desire; they come apart at the price tag.* With everything you want to achieve there is a price tag. As long as the price tag is acceptable, you will move forward. BUT, if the price is too great, you will find a reason to not continue. Time and time again I have had people tell me what they want for their life, develop a plan, then discover the price tag and walk away. Their thought is *this is more than I am willing to pay for this part of my life.*

Here is the other side I find interesting. The more successful a person becomes, the greater the fear of loss. When they are just starting out and there is nothing to lose, they are willing to take the risk necessary to keep the journey moving. Then, when they start to achieve the success, they become protective of what they have obtained.

I love asking people: *If you saw something you wanted, but you would have to risk all you have to obtain it, would you?*

The most common response I get is *NO!* The reasons given are:

- *I've worked too hard to get where I am.*
- *I don't think I have the energy to do this again.*
- *I like things the way they are now.*
- *I have others who now depend on me.*

Boil all this down and you are dealing with the *Fear of Loss.* When a person is no longer willing to take a risk, they slip into the emotional status of protecting what they think they have. In that posture they lose the creative edge that took them to where they are now. When you lose that creative edge, you are trapped in the Circle of Sameness. In that circle you start the process that will cost you the joy of success.

Over and over I have listened to people talk about how much more fun it was to achieve than it is to protect. So much of protective behavior is negative. It feeds yesterday; it doesn't nourish today. When yesterday is all you are staring at, you become a hostage to those things you have obtained. You are no longer planning today to be prepared for tomorrow. You are now working to keep what you have; even if it means losing the joy that came with achieving it.

The Fear of Loss can take a dream driven person and turn them into a skeptic. It can make them spend more time thinking about what others want, rather than what they can offer those in their life.

The Fear of Loss can take a dreamer and turn them into one who is controlled by worry. They are constantly worrying about what "might happen," rather than enjoying the abundance of their life.

The Fear of Loss can take a proactive person and turn them into a reactor. Rather than continuing the search for improvement, they now work to make sure they don't lose what they have obtained.

Now, the tapes are driven by the negative, not the positive. Now, this person is a hostage to where they have been; they don't have a plan for continuing to improve. They spend their time talking about how tough it was to get where they are; they spend their time fearful of each event, rather than finding the challenge that it offers their life.

The Fear of Loss is about living in the shade afraid if they step into the sunlight, they might get burned. They really enjoy the sunlight, but the fear keeps them staring at all that is wrong. Now they have become a shell of the person they once were. They are a history book that has written the last chapter of their growth. The tapes are all about yesterday. They now exist to protect what they have.

The Fear of Success:

If I do what I know I should do, I might receive rewards I don't deserve.

Does this one sound strange to you? Why would anyone feel they don't deserve good in their life? It is all about the tapes they have chosen to play. Have you ever watched someone get close to what they have said they wanted for their life and then, sabotage it?

I understand this behavior. I lived it for several years. I am a very driven person. BUT, drive without self worth is a dangerous combination. Your drive takes you to the edge of success, but then the negative tapes about who you are and what you should have in life kick in. At this point you design a plan to fulfill your negative personal picture. You will make sure you defeat yourself. Then, the tapes of blame and guilt kick in. Each time you sabotage your life it becomes easier to do it the next time. Soon, you will believe you don't deserve good things in your life. *Why, look at what has happened.*

61

You worked so hard to achieve good things and then they fell apart around you.

All behavior is tied to an agenda.

There is no mention of how you designed the actions that made sure you didn't succeed. There is no mention of your self destructive behavior. You must learn that *all behavior is tied to an agenda.* I listen to what people say, but I pay attention to what they do. I have learned that most people are a contradiction. Their words contradict their behavior. They say one thing and then act out another. Since the behavior is more profound than their words, study the actions. That is the real agenda the person is living.

Don't forget, *all human lives collide at the point of agendas.* There are no coincidences in a human life. All behavior is the result of your personal agenda. You are perfectly designed to achieve what you are achieving. There is no one to blame; there is no one to point your finger at. You make choices that are acted out through behaviors. Those behaviors create journeys that have consequences.

Twice I sabotaged relationships that I said were important to me. I was always talking about wanting a strong romantic relationship in my life. I would meet someone, have the relationship move forward and when things got to the point of moving toward marriage, I would sabotage it. I just didn't feel I deserved this in my life. The old tapes were still so strong that I couldn't believe that someone could love me for me. There had to be a hidden agenda. I would let these old tapes take over the direction of the relationship. I would let my fear of deserving a successful relationship take control. Know what? I ruined things!

I remember several years ago when I met Karen. She was introduced to me by a mutual acquaintance. We hit it off and after several months of dating I asked her to marry me. We were progressing when the old tapes kicked in. I can remember how I started playing those tapes where my mother would tell me *I was not a lovable person. I would never have anyone in my life who would truly love me.*

Those tapes were so powerful! They created behaviors in me that were designed to sabotage what Karen and I had. And, you know what? It worked. I chased Karen out of my life.

Then, there was Kim. I met Kim while I was in Dallas. She had gone through a very traumatic time in her life. We hit it off and I just knew she was the person for my life. Even her parents liked me.

Again, marriage plans were made. Again, those old negative tapes kicked in. Again, I designed a process that would sabotage the relationship. And once again, it worked. I just couldn't seem to get past the feeling I didn't deserve a successful happy relationship.

Three years after my relationship with Kim ended I met Karen Cummins. I had told myself I would not repeat those old tapes. I had spent a lot of personal time working through the scripts that were still present in my emotional life. I will say it to you again. *I don't care how strong you are mentally and emotionally; there are certain old negative tapes that can always get to you.*

Karen and I dated long distance and did okay. I finally asked her to move to Florida. I would put her to work in my company. This would allow us to see if we really could make it together. In reality I wondered if I could get beyond my sabotaging of personal relationships.

Karen was so patient. I explained to her my past struggles and how I wanted this to work. We became engaged, but setting a wedding date was something I struggled with. We would talk about it; we would talk about our life together; we would talk about my fears. Karen would say to me over and over *I am not like the others you have had in your life. I love you for you, not who you are.*

I would hear what she was saying, but each time she would say it the old tapes would be triggered. My emotions would take over and those negative fears would grow stronger. I knew what I was doing. I was repeating those "Old Behaviors" that had sabotaged my past relationships. I was doing it all over again.

The wake up call came when I arrived back in my hotel room and found a Fed Ex letter from Karen. Inside was a note from her telling me she was moving back home to Virginia. She could no longer handle my unwillingness to make a full commitment. I immediately picked up the phone and called home to hear only the ringing of the phone. I reached her on her car phone. Her dad had come from Virginia, helped her pack her stuff and they were driving back to Virginia. I have never forgotten her words.

I love you very much, but I can't live this way any longer. I have given you every opportunity to get beyond all your problems. I have been patient. I have believed if I could just hang in, things will change. I don't believe any more that they will. I have to get on with my life.

To this day I can remember the emotions I went through. It was like that night when I was sixteen all over again. My first response was to blame Karen. *Why couldn't she understand. I wanted to marry her, but there was this stuff I had to work through. How many times had I told her what I wanted.*

Then, came this feeling of rejection. *My mother was right. I will never have a loving relationship. I guess I have to accept that fact and know I will be alone.*

Then there was the feeling of failure. *Well, you did it again! You have managed to sabotage another relationship. No matter how hard you try, you can't make one last.*

There was also the feeling of abandonment. *How could she just pick up and leave. If she really loved me, she wouldn't do that to me.*

Two days later I arrived back in the Palm Beaches. I walked in the house and immediately felt the loss. Everywhere I turned there was this empty feeling. Where her things had once been, there was nothing. I sat and just stared at the empty corners of my life.

I was no longer angry at Karen. I knew she did what I had designed to happen. My old tapes had pushed her back to Virginia. For the first time I really felt an empty feeling I had never felt before.

In Denver I had handled the relationship by making Karen the issue. I had never really faced my own behavior.

In Dallas I had handled the relationship by making Kim the issue. Again, I never faced my own behavior.

This time, as hard as I tried, I couldn't do that. The old tapes would flip on but I was so angry at the "Old Me" I refused to listen. I wasn't going to have this chapter end as the previous chapters had ended. I was going to face my behavior and if this relationship ended, it wouldn't be because I had chased Karen back to Virginia.

I called Karen and asked if I could come to Virginia so the two of us could talk about this. This was like going to my parents house and confronting the situation. Only this time, I called before I went. Through that phone call and visit I was able to start the process of putting those old tapes away. Seven months later Karen and I finally were married. Our relationship is not perfect, but I am a blessed man to have her in my life.

I remember Karen telling me *I never thought you would call. I figured you would just close the door and go on your merry way.* The "Old Me" would have done that. In fact, I came close to doing just that. This time rather than giving in to the old tapes that had programmed the "Old Me," I faced the situation. In facing the negative fears I was able to rise above and move beyond the yesterdays I was repeating.

Do you understand this? Do you understand the power that negative fear has over your life? Do you see how easy it is to just give in, move deeper into your personal prison and remain there behind the self constructed bars?

You don't have to live there! You don't have to allow negative fear to make you a prisoner in your own life. You can get beyond this.

The process has four steps to it:

Step 1 • *Face what is really happening in your life.*

Step 2 • *Redesign the behaviors that have made it okay.*

Step 3 • *Strengthen the good things about you.*

Step 4 • *Reach out to others who are there to make you better.*

The great challenge is realizing the power the "Old You" has in your life. The great awareness is to understand how much of your life is defined by the old negative tapes you continue to play. The turning point is when you can shout as loud as you can shout *"Old You," sit down and shut up! I will no longer be controlled by your presence. I will no longer surrender my life to your program.*

Inside of each of us there is a "New You" waiting to get out. Inside there is a "New You" ready to show you a today that is better than any yesterday you have ever lived. Inside of each there is this "New You" who understands that life is about finding inner happiness, personal fulfillment and freedom. Those are the things that await you when you can let go of yesterday's negative tapes.

Chapter 4
THE PROCESS

When a person doesn't understand the process that brings growth to their life, they continue to wander in their Circle of Sameness.

People ask me constantly *aren't you angry over your childhood?* There was a period of time when I was very angry. That was before I had worked through the emotions that had been stored. During this journey, I learned *anger results when you don't face what is happening.* Anger is a reaction; it is not a response. When you choose to run from and not face what is happening, you will build anger. When you choose to run from and not face what is happening, you will blame others for what is.

When I faced those emotions, I was able to release my anger. At that time I realized my childhood was a blessing. It has made me who I am today. Working through that part of my life has allowed me to see the lessons that I needed to learn. Many times when I tell my story, people come to me and say *my childhood was much like yours. I only wish I could be like you. I still struggle with what happened in my life.*

Everyone has a story. Everyone has a past. Everyone is the result of what they have done with where

69

they have been. Each day is either a repeat of yesterday or an opportunity to take what you have learned and improve who you are and where you are headed.

For many years my life was a repeat. I was held hostage by all the negative tapes I played from my childhood. Inside I wanted to break free; inside I wanted to get beyond the pain and confusion. Yet, those old tapes were such a controlling force. Each time I would get close to breaking free, the tapes would turn on and beat back my desire. Each time I would get the inner courage to step forward, they were there to create an emotional roadblock that would knock me backward. As much as I worked to move forward, I was an emotional hostage in my own life.

This is the greatest challenge I see faced by those I meet. I sit, I listen, I watch, and I see lives with talent that are wasting away from the inability to break free of the "Old Self."

That "Old Self" has the power to steal their happiness. Oh, it will let them experience moments of happiness, but then slap that person with a negative tape that takes their happiness away. When that happens, the old tapes kick on and the message is very simple *I don't deserve happiness in my life.*

That "Old Self" has the ability to take personal fulfillment from their life. These people spend each day as a slave in a life they really don't enjoy. They go to work and when they arrive their spirit dies as they enter.

Work is something they do, not something they really enjoy. Many people have told me *what I am doing is not my dream. I do this because it pays the bills. If I could live my dream my life would be different.* What happens is each time their mind begins to play with their dream, the old tapes kick in and cloud the picture with doubts and fears. The dream slips back into the dark corner of their imagination and they move forward in their world designed for mere existence.

Many go home to lifeless relationships. They are just there. They exist under the same roof, but there is little there that brings fulfillment to their life. They share common space, not a common dream.

That "Old Self" also has the ability to remove "freedom" from their vocabulary. When a life lacks happiness and the feeling of personal fulfillment, it becomes a slave in a world of limited thought. Without a sense of freedom a person only sees what they fear. Without a sense of personal freedom a person moves to protect what they think they have and refuses to take the risk necessary to move beyond the thoughts of yesterday. Therefore, today becomes a repeat of yesterday, and each day their life finds its willingness to explore, its desire to seek, its belief in something better just getting weaker and weaker. In the long run they just give up and accept what is as what will be. This removes success from their thoughts and makes failure a negative that results in defeat.

I was asked recently, *how many people do you feel really break out of their Circle of Sameness and live their potential?*

My reply left the group with a stunned look on their faces. *Only 1% of people ever break free and reach their potential.*

Think about it! How many people do you know who really have happiness in their life? I know a lot who are searching for it, but as far as having it in their life, I can not name many.

How many people do you know who have achieved personal fulfillment? Think about it! How many can you name? I know many who have a job, who have 'things', but will still tell you their life lacks that feeling of personal fulfillment. I know many who exist in relationships, but don't find what they thought a relationship would offer.

How many people do you know who really live with a sense of freedom? Freedom is the ability to live your life the way you want without having to be what others expect or plan for you to be. How many do you know? Most are busy trying to impress, live up to others' expectations or trying to be what they are not. Each day they dress their life with behaviors designed to please others. Each day they show up looking around to see what others need for them to be. Each day they are simply an actor in someone else's play. They have no freedom. They are because others expect them to be.

I know the truth to all of this. That was how I lived for years. I was fearful of others not liking me, so I played their game. I was fearful of not having anyone in my life, so I allowed them to write the rules. I was fearful of not being able to measure up to their expectations, so I stayed in my comfort zone. I didn't think I deserved good in my life, so I would make sure I never got the reward I was seeking.

Now, when I look back at how I lived, it paints a very depressing picture. I wasn't me! I was a person creating moments of existence, rather than one who was enjoying life. My behavior was designed to make sure I didn't offend; my speech was always about saying the right thing; my existence was about creating moments without pain. Little did I know I was dying from the inside out. Little did I realize I was getting up each day with a design to waste my life. I was a person who only saw life from the outside. I didn't understand what it meant to live with purpose. I didn't understand what it meant to live from the inside out.

Oh, I was like so many; I wrote my goals. I didn't write them to achieve them; I wrote them because others said you had to have them. They weren't meaningful statements. They were just words that created another lie for me to convince myself of.

I've got to tell you, I became great at lying to myself. I would feed my mind these stories of what I was going to do. I would tell others what I wanted to achieve with my life. In reality, there was no way I was going to do any of that. It sounded good and it made me appear as a "together" person. BUT, on the inside I was lost, struggling and searching for "ME." The person I knew was the composite of what others had told me about me.

The real picture I had of me was one of a boy:
- who wasn't lovable.
- who wasn't wanted.
- who wasn't very smart.
- who really shouldn't be alive.
- whose life was a total screw up.

This made me very skeptical of anyone who approached my life with kindness and wanted to help me. I would emotionally run away; I would mentally question what they really wanted. I was actually fearful of kindness and accepting of pain. Have you ever known someone like that?

It took me years to learn to trust people; it took me years to believe in me. It took me years to free myself from yesterday's tape library. The process was not taught me by others. It was one I worked out on my own.

I tried counseling and learned something very interesting. Too many counselors don't want you to get healthy. If you get healthy, you are no longer their patient. The key is to tie you to them for years and keep you struggling with the same issue. I have met people who have gone to counselors for years and are really no further along in their life. Too many times counseling is just another form of being a hostage. It really is easy to tie a person to you through the pain that keeps reappearing in their life.

If a person wants to get better, the process is simple, yet complex. It involves four steps, and they have to come in one order.

Each step demands a little more from you.
- *Face what is really happening in your life.*
- *Redesign the behaviors that have made it okay.*
- *Strengthen the good things about you.*
- *Reach out to others who are there to make you better.*

That doesn't look too challenging, does it? It is the most challenging journey you will ever take. It requires a redefining of your life. This is not about outside-in living. This is about inside-out living.

Outside-in living views life from the expectations of others. It makes the opinions and wishes of others more important than those you have for yourself. It is about moving yourself up on your own personal food chain.

Living from the inside out is about making yourself a priority in your own life. It is about getting your priorities straight. It is about you being free to live your dream, rather than living the life others program for you.

When Karen and I got married one of the conversations we had was about how she would fit into my life. I think one of the most unhealthy things we talk about is *making another person #1 in your life.* That is the creator of so much of the strife in marriage. It creates a relationship based on "need" not "want." So many divorces occur because of this. Many who marry don't do so out of love; they do it out of need! They "need" someone in their life. They really aren't looking for love; they are looking for someone to accept them. This creates an emotional collision from the very beginning. They judge the "love" of the other person based on what they do for them.

You see, if two people marry out of "need," the only value the other has is in meeting their needs. As long as "needs" are being met, things are great. BUT, when the "needs" are not being met, it creates a family of negative emotions:

- *You don't love me anymore!*
- *I'm not important to your life anymore.*
- *All you wanted me for was sex!*

When you sit with couples and listen to their struggles, you see this very clearly. The struggles are there because the expectations were based on one fulfilling the other's needs. The collision was planned from the very beginning.

This also becomes one of the major sources of punishment. *Well, if you are not going to do that for me, I am not going to do anything for you.* This adds to the negative emotions and fuels the war that is designed to destroy the other person. This moves the struggles from pain to torture. At this level the agenda becomes destruction, not solution.

Before Karen and I got married, I felt it was only fair I shared with her her position in my life. I told her *you will never be #1 in my life. If you need to be #1 in my life, this relationship won't work. I promise you will always be #3 on my list of priorities.*

Number 1 in my life is my relationship with my God. That is critical to me. I must keep that relationship strong. Number 2 is my relationship with me. If I don't have a strong relationship with me, I will use Karen as my emotional whipping post. Number 3 is Karen. When my life is solid from the inside-out, our relationship just gets better and better.

When your life is driven from the outside-in, life is designed around the events you are living at that moment. It makes life a series of ups and downs. In that pattern of living you are never sure who is going to walk through the front door. With that pattern you remain a stranger to yourself and to all who share your life with you.

All people live their life either from the outside-in or from the inside-out. Those who are growing and achieving their potential have chosen to live from the inside-out. These comprise the 1%. They have moved beyond their negative fears; they are writing the script they live by each day; they are moving at a manageable pace; they have the discipline necessary to maintain their focus and not be controlled by the negatives that go on around them. These are the people who have learned to live the process of being better, smarter and taller in their life.

The Process Explained

Personal growth is not an accident! It is not something that just happens. It is the result of a person who understands disciplined consistency. It is the result of a person who is living consistent persistency balanced with persistent consistency.

Have you ever watched someone struggle with losing weight? They have tried diet after diet. They buy into any program that promises to make them into a thinner person. BUT, they still struggle with losing weight. The challenge they face is their lack of disciplined consistency. They start dieting, come face to face with negative fear and revert to past behavior.

The desire is there, but what is lacking is the

disciplined consistency to handle the old tapes they listen to. Tapes that say:
- *You will never be thin!*
- *You've tried this before and failed.*
- *You couldn't do it then and you can't do it now.*

Have you ever watched a person struggle from one relationship to another? Each relationship starts with high hopes and ends in disaster. The challenge they face is their inability to get beyond their old tapes. If you study the type of person they bring into their life, it is the same unhealthy person they just got rid of, just in a new body. What they lack is the disciplined consistency to face what they have designed their life to achieve.

Have you ever watched a person move from job to job? They can't seem to fit in. They are constantly unhappy with what they are doing. Nothing is ever right with their job. They are in a constant searching for the perfect job, yet they have no idea what they want for their life. What they lack is an understanding of the process that will take their life beyond what it has been.

Step 1: Face What Is

Most people are designed to repeat, not improve. When you study human behavior, you discover that most people spend their life denying, not taking responsibility for the events of their life.

Any human who doesn't want to face what is, can find someone or something to blame. Blame is one of the top forms of escape. As long as someone or something else is responsible for their condition, they don't have to take responsibility for their behavior. That has become a lifestyle in our country today. Look around you! Look at all the times where rather than stepping up and taking responsibility for what a person has done, they look around for something and/or someone to blame.

Our society has become one of non-accountable people. Listen to people talk, study the justice system, watch the behavior of people and you see person after person who has chosen to deny responsibility for their behavior and place blame on something or someone. This design only makes humans emotionally weaker and mentally more unhealthy.

You are perfectly designed to achieve what you are achieving!

Facing what is means taking responsibility for the design of your life. One of my top philosophies of life is *you are perfectly designed to achieve what you are achieving.* I could have spent my entire life blaming my mother for all the negatives in my life. Believe me, for a while I did just that. She was my reason for all the ills of my life. Over a period of time I realized I was just traveling in a vicious circle. Nothing was getting better. I was just emotionally sinking deeper and deeper into a hole designed to force me to repeat, not improve.

It was Spencer Hayes who helped me to understand blame is a hostage taker. The longer you place blame the longer you have to remain a hostage to the situations of yesterday. When you accept responsibility for your life's direction, you realize you have to face what is.

I couldn't go back and change yesterday. It was a fact! I couldn't change what had happened, but I could make sure I didn't continue that journey. I had the right to move beyond my yesterday. To do that I had to face my behavior. Up to that point all I had done was feast on my mother's behavior. She was all I had chosen to look at. Yet, she wasn't my life; she was only part of my life. She was part of my journey. If I chose, she could continue to rule my life. If I chose, I could grow beyond her. It was my choice. I was perfectly designed to achieve with my life whatever I wanted to achieve.

The challenge for many is they get so hung up with what went wrong, they can't see beyond it. If that is all the sight they have, it is what they are designed to repeat. If they are an emotional hostage to a yesterday they keep coloring with negative emotions, then today will be a repeat performance. That is a choice they make. It is not something someone else does to them. It is a choice they make each day and then, act out with behaviors.

The first step to getting beyond the negative tapes of yesterday is to *face the fact it happened!* Blame is not facing the fact; it is a form of avoiding the issue. Facing it means admitting it has happened and denying the event the right to continue to rule your life.

Facing what is means *confronting the fears that are attached to it.* Remember the five fears we talked about earlier?

- Fear of Abandonment: *If I do what I know I need to do, I might be left alone.*

- Fear of Rejection: *If I do what I know I need to do, someone might not like it.*

- Fear of Failure: *If I do what I know I need to do, it might expose the fact I can't do it.*

- Fear of Loss: *If I do what I know I need to do, it might cost me more mentally, emotionally or financially than I am willing to pay.*

- Fear of Success: *If I do what I know I need to do, it might reward me with things I don't deserve in my life.*

To face what is and move beyond it you must understand the place of these five fears in your life and face them head on. The longer you let these linger in your life the more control they take of your life. This is where the Old You goes when it wants to make sure you remain a prisoner in your own life. These fears are all designed to force you to relive yesterday. These fears are all there to make sure you replay the tapes you made about the situation. Those tapes are negative!

The first step to getting beyond your yesterday tapes is *to face what is*. This is where the challenge begins. Yet, within this four step process this is the easiest of the steps.

Step 2: Redesign What Has Been

In the first step you had to face the emotions you have tied to situations. Now, you have to do something about those emotions. Facing an emotion and then doing something about it is a challenging journey.

I have worked with many who were willing to face and admit the event, but when you ask them to step forward and redesign their behavior, you can see the fear race through their eyes. Redesigning the behavior means admitting your fear, being held accountable for the behavior and moving beyond making someone else the reason your life is the way it is. That is a challenge!

Have you noticed how many people feel that admitting their fears is a negative? For some reason they believe you should be inwardly strong enough to handle fear. The "Old You" wants you to believe that. It knows that negative fear is an energy zapper; it knows negative fear blocks your mind's ability to show you the pathway through it; it knows negative fear locks you into constantly reliving the event in order to justify what you are not doing. Each of these makes it impossible for you to improve. Without the improvement you are a hostage to whatever negative emotions you have brought into that event.

You have to redesign the emotions you have attached to the event. That means going back and reviewing the event. It means going back and rewriting the script that you have written. Every negative event you have hung onto has a script that goes with it. That script is emotional. Each time you turn the old tape on you are listening to the script you have written for that event. Each time it is the same tape replaying the same story. Each time you listen to it, you grow a little more accepting of it as a natural part of your life.

Your life is a series of scripts you play over and over.

To get beyond it you have to rescript the event. Your life is simply a series of scripts you play over and over. These scripts trigger feelings which are translated into behaviors which are acted out.

I understand how this works. Before I had faced and redesigned my emotional connections with my mother, if you mentioned her name or let a similar situation happen the old tapes would automatically turn on. When they did, I was sucked back into all the negative emotions that were tied to those events. It would create a downward spiral. I don't care how much progress I had made; it just reversed the direction and sent me backward into an emotional tail spin. Do you have any idea what that did to my "New Self?" Here I was racing backward; here I was reliving what I thought I had moved beyond; here I was once again face to face with all those negative emotions. It was as if my mother was right there in front of me once again playing her games with my life.

I would get angry with me! I would hate her a little more. I would begin to believe there was no way of getting beyond my yesterday. That is not only a form of depression, but a form of solitary confinement in my personal prison of yesterday's pain.

Only when I faced the fact, addressed my fears and had a desire that was stronger than my pain, could I redesign what had been. I am not saying it was easy. It wasn't! It was frightening; it was painful; it required all the mental energy I had. Each time my old emotional tapes would turn on I had to mentally fight going back and replaying all those old negative tapes.

At that point I had to make a choice. I could allow the old tapes to play and control the emotions I was applying to the event I was reliving, or I could choose to turn the tape off. To do that I had to have a mental presence that was stronger than my emotional presence.

In the beginning I couldn't get beyond the emotional tapes. I wanted to, but at that point the "Old Me" was just too strong. Every time I would work to get beyond the "Old Me," he would raise his ugly head and throw something even more negative at me. It took time and persistent consistency to win the battle. I had to fight and have a lot of vocal conversations with my "Old Self." I mean I had to talk to myself out loud.

Many think this is foolish, but to get beyond your negative yesterdays you have to be strong enough to face the fact the Old You exists. Only by having the strength can you start redesigning the journey. You have to confront the Old You vocally out loud.

Have you ever had a conversation in your head and it not have the impact you wanted it to have? The reason is *you don't listen to conversations in your head!* They are simply like a thought that passes through your mind. When you talk to yourself out loud, you hear what you are saying. The power here is talking to your "Old Self" just as if you were having a conversation with someone standing before you.

Talking out loud helped me to hear what I was saying. Once I started listening, I heard all the negative things I was saying. I've got to tell you I was saying some terrible things about my mother and about me. The most dangerous was not what I was saying about my mother, but what I was saying about myself. That was where the damage was happening. My mother was the reason for the conversation, but I was the focal point. Each negative thought I had about myself just made me mentally and emotionally weaker. The weaker I became the easier it was for the "Old Me" to maintain self. Listening to myself made it possible for me to start rescripting the story.

To rescript I had to find the lesson that was hidden in the event. This is where I find so many trapped.

Old tapes are not about lessons; they are about replaying negative tapes.

The old negative tapes are not about a lesson; they are about replaying the pain associated with the event. As long as you are replaying the tape of pain, that is where you must stay. Your emotional understandings about the event create the picture your mind draws of what happened. As long as those sketches are about pain, you feed all the negative feelings you have dragged around inside yourself.

Dragging all those negative tapes through your life is how the "Old You" holds you hostage to your yesterday. Only when you can throw those old negative tapes away can you free yourself from the pattern you have used to live in today. Doing that means changing the sketch. It means facing the event and rather than looking for the pain, searching for the lesson. Without a lesson there is no freedom from your old negative yesterday tapes.

Wrapped up in every event in your life is a lesson. It does not just appear. You have to search for it. The "Old You" doesn't want you to find the lesson; the "Old You" wants you to relive the pain. The "Old You" knows when you find the lesson, you are free from the pain. That means you are free from the control the "Old You" has had over your life. Your reliving yesterday's pain is the major way the "Old You" holds you hostage.

When I was finally strong enough to face the plan the "Old Me" was using to hold me a hostage in my own life, I got angry. To overcome what the "Old Me" was doing all I had to do was find the lesson. I thought this would be simple, but it wasn't. I had to change my emotional thinking pattern. For years when the situation played in my mind, I would turn on the old negative tapes. At first I would tell myself *I would view events from the negative. I would slow down and work to find the lesson.* Each time I tried, the "Old Me" would turn up the heat. The "Old Me" would reach deep into the event and throw emotions at me that would drag me negatively back. When this happened, I was sucked into the old behavior and *I would emotionally speed up!*

I finally realized that was the technique. Each time I would speed up I would lose the ability to control my thinking about the event. Each time I would speed up I just got sucked deeper into my negative feelings. Redefining my behavior started with realizing I needed to mentally and emotionally slow down.

I had conversation after conversation with my "Old Self." Each time I would tell the "Old Me" *you can't do this to me any longer. I know how you work. You want me to emotionally speed up. I won't play your game anymore.*

Each time I finished those words I would take a deep breath and ask my mind to show me what I had learned from this event in my life. The answers didn't come automatically. I had to keep slowing myself down.

I kept a Personal Growth Journal. With each event I faced, I would note the date and the emotions I was feeling. Writing this down helped me to understand even more the program the "Old Me" was using to hold me as a hostage. Writing my emotions also helped me find the lesson contained in the event.

The other strength this provided was a reference point to understand how the "Old Me" attacked. Each time I defeated the "Old Me," he didn't just go away. He would get angry and come after me with another event.

The beginning events were easy to find the lessons. BUT, as I peeled the layers away, the events got more challenging. Each time I won one battle, the "Old Me" was there with the next.

It was at this point I learned *life is a series of layered events.* Each event you don't want to face simply creates another situation. That situation is stacked on top of the one you still haven't faced. To get out of your emotional prison you have to take it apart layer by layer.

This takes time, persistency and patience. This is why so many ask *is there no end to all of this?* Yes, there is an end, but not until you get to the bottom issue. If you stop before you get to the core issue, you just start the emotional stacking all over again. The key is your willingness to take the time, maintain the persistence and have the patience to continue even when you feel things are not happening fast enough.

Again, understand how powerful and intelligent the "Old You" is. The "Old You" knows your eagerness to get through; the "Old You" knows you *just want to get on with your life.* At this point you are very vulnerable. At this point the tendency is to be impatient. So, at this point the "Old You" steps up the attacks with thoughts like:

- *See, I told you you can't do this!*
- *This isn't going to work; you know that!*
- *This is too much for you to handle!*

All of these are designed to challenge your patience. If you lose your patience, you will not be willing to take the time and have the persistence to get through the event. That is why time, persistency and patience are the keys to getting to the lesson.

The second step in the process of freeing yourself from yesterday's tapes is redesigning what has been.

Step 3: Strengthen The Things That Make You Good

The third step is critical to freeing yourself from the negatives of yesterday. When you are trapped in the negatives of yesterday, you lose sight of what is right with your life. That means the only pictures your mind has to view are the negative tapes the "Old You" keeps emotionally replaying. Since there is such a large library of these tapes, your emotions can continue to search the library until it finds the one that works in this situation.

Whatever you do, don't underestimate the power of the "Old You." It is your arch enemy who is designed to keep you as a prisoner in your own life.

I can remember all the negative beliefs I had about myself. Those old tapes were really powerful. Each time I looked in the mirror all I saw was a person who must be really terrible. After all his mother didn't want him, and then the people who adopted him didn't want him either. I can remember nights when I was 17 & 18 crying myself to sleep. I would crawl into bcd, pull the covers over my head and just cry. I was so lonely and just wanted someone to hold me and tell me everything was okay. Instead I had this tape playing over and over in my head. It was my mother shouting at me about what a

91

terrible person I was. It was my mother pointing her finger and making one of her three constantly repeated statements:

- *Don't you ever forget that your mother didn't want you.*

- *You know, we really didn't have to adopt you.*

- *You are one of the dumbest people I have ever met.*

I couldn't turn the tape off. It seemed to have its own switch, and I had no control over it. I would scream at my mother to shut up, but the tape would continue to play. The message just kept playing — *you are a terrible person.*

What do you think you would remember about your childhood if that was what you heard the majority of the time? What kinds of behaviors do you think you would have in your life? Do you think this would affect your self confidence?

For the longest time I didn't bother to think about any strengths I might have. My life was simply about replaying the tapes my mother had so graciously programed me with. Each time I strived to see beyond them, the "Old Me" would raise his ugly head and frighten me with an experience from my yesterday. At this point in my journey the tapes were filled with the fear of abandonment and rejection.

There were people who tried to help me, but the tapes about being abandoned again wouldn't let me allow them into my life. *After all if your mother and father didn't want you, what makes you think a total stranger would treat you any differently?*

There were those who offered me their friendship, but those tapes about rejection came through loud and clear. *Why would they want to be my friend? It could only be for one reason and that was to hurt me. I was not going to go through this again.*

This forced me to withdraw into myself. I became a loner and lost myself in my schooling and my work.

The change in the tapes came from three or four people who kept working to get through my defenses. I had layers of gates around me. Each gate had a series of locks on it. Oh, I would let you into the outer, outer, outer courtyard, but no closer.

Troy Howell was the gentleman who came to me the morning after my father left me on the sidewalk. He and his wife, Pearl, were always there for me. Pearl would hug me each time she saw me. In church I would sit with their family and it felt good, but there was still the reality that I had to go home by myself. I would eat meals at their house. I would laugh and cut up with their family, but then it was time for me to go back to my little dark room. To this day I still remember them and smile. They will never know the impact they had on my life. Troy, Pearl and Gayla are a big reason I made it through. This family would later on be a catalyst to me challenging my mother's tapes.

There was J.C. Luke. What a great man. He was the owner of Luke's IGA in Ardmore, Oklahoma. When my mother informed me I had to pay room and board, it was Mr. Luke who gave me a job. When he learned what had happened, he stepped up his presence in my life. There were times when I didn't like him. He was always there to confront my behavior. He was so funny. He had a unique way of asking you questions that looked right through you. He always made me accountable for what I said I would do. I think Mr. Luke and Arlie, the produce manager, had designed this plan they were using on my life.

Arlie was a real clown. He could make you laugh and laugh. He had names for his different varieties of produce. He would do shows with the vegetables. I would be in the back room pouting from one of Mr. Luke's appearances and Arlie would bring a cucumber, carrot or some other vegetable over and do one of his shows. His presence was important, and little did he know he would be part of me challenging my mother's tapes.

Mr. Luke was a rock. He was fair; he was ethical; he was firm. He was always willing to challenge my negative statements. He wouldn't let me beat myself up. I soon learned *if I said anything negative and he heard it, I was going to be challenged.* Little did he realize that his presence would be part of my facing the emotional tapes I was playing.

Then, there was Spencer Hayes from the Southwestern Bible Company. He was the turning point in my life. I still pause and thank God for bringing him into my life when he did. That night when he looked me in the eyes and said *you have got to stop beating yourself up* still rings in my mind.

How could a total stranger know that about me. Was I that transparent? I guess so. Later, I learned that Spencer had gone through his own journey and saw himself in me. His presence in my life challenged me mentally, forced me to emotionally look at myself and face all those tapes I had accepted as real.

He pushed me mentally, he challenged me emotionally and he forced me to stop and listen to what I was thinking and saying. He had this uncanny way of always calling at the right time. It was as if he knew when the "Old Me" was fighting for control of my life. Most of the time it was his calls that allowed the "New Me" to tell the "Old Me" to *shut up!* I can still feel his gentle presence guiding me to some point of personal understanding that showed me a strength, rather than a weakness. It was Spencer who showed me the need to confront my mom and dad. It was Spencer Hayes who fortified me with the strength to make that trip to their house and start the next chapter in my life.

Up until that visit, my life had only one chapter. That chapter was about self destruction. It was about letting one person completely rule my life. It was about only seeing the wrongs and only experiencing the negative emotions.

When I left my parent's house, I now had a second chapter to write. That chapter was about freedom. That chapter was about realizing there was more than one way to view the events of life.

There are so many people who never get beyond Chapter 1. Each day they just add more pages to their biography of self destruction. As long as they continue to play the negative tapes of yesterday, they will only have one chapter. So many people go to their grave never having realized there was more than one chapter.

Then there was Clyde Irving. Clyde was my sales manager during the summers I sold Bible Books for the Southwestern Bible Company. He really became like a brother to me. I could talk to him about things I could not talk about to anyone else. He was ten years older than me, but was never too busy to listen. He would never tell me what to do, but would show me the options I had. Then, he would walk me through each option and let me make my own decision. I can't remember a conversation we had where I left without having a plan of action.

I can still hear him say *what good is it to talk about what needs to be done and then leave without doing it.* He would have me choose an action plan and set a date by which I would have it done. That was one of the most powerful lessons anyone ever taught me.

Each of these men, Troy Howell, J.C. Luke, Spencer Hayes and Clyde Irving added to my life. Each of these men taught me about my strengths. Each denied me the right to hang onto the pains I was dragging out of yesterday. Each forced me to see my strengths and start using them.

It is amazing what happens when you start letting go of the wrongs and seeing the rights. It is amazing how much freedom the "New You" brings to your life when you give it control. All of a sudden there are good things happening; all of a sudden there are things to celebrate; all of a sudden the old negative tapes don't have such an impact on your life.

Through the process your worries slowly turn to calmness. Through the process your doubts are replaced with clarity. Through the process your uncertainties give way to confidence. With these three in place you begin to see a better you. The more you get to celebrate this "New You" the easier it becomes to control the old negative tapes.

Don't get me wrong. This doesn't happen overnight. It is a process where you have to face one situation at a time and redesign it with lessons. If you are looking for the quick fix, this isn't it. It has taken me years to turn the old tapes off and learn how to play the tapes filled with successes. It really has taken time, consistent persistency and patience. Yes, I have slipped at times, but when you start developing a pattern of success, it is easier to get through the valleys.

Today, I am one of the strongest internal people you will ever meet. I throw parties and I am the only one I invite. You should hear the celebration; you should witness the fun there is in getting beyond the old tapes that only have one purpose — *to hold you a hostage in your life.*

Step 4: Reach Out To Others Who Can Make You Better

This final step cannot be achieved until you get through the first three. I have had people come to me for help before they ever really faced the fact they had a problem. They come looking for the quick fix, not a solution that will close the door on being held hostage.

So many times they have said to me *I know this is going to take time, but couldn't we speed it up.*

My response is always the same. *NO! It has taken you years to get to this point and it will take time to learn how to turn the old negative tapes off.*

We have all heard the old adage *when the pupil is ready, the teacher will appear.* It is true, but many aren't looking for the teacher. They are looking for the wizard with his little bag of magic dust. They want the wizard to sprinkle it on them and for all things to be fine in a flash. That is not the way it works.

The process is about slowing down and facing the real issues. It is about your willingness to stop fighting what needs to be done and redesign the behavioral process you are using in your life. It is about you learning how to quit beating yourself up. It is about finding your strengths and using them as the foundation for your personal growth. It is about managing the pace of your life so you are aware of those who are walking the same journey. Some may be beside you and some may be in front of you, but their presence can strengthen your journey. These people won't push to spend time with you; they will make you aware of their presence, but you must reach out to them.

Reaching out involves confidence in yourself. Many people who lack confidence are fearful of those who are where they want to be. To justify the fear they must work to tear these people down. This is just the "Old Self" winning another battle.

When you reach out to another your confidence will allow you to see the value they bring to your life. It will allow you to see why they are there and what each of you offers the other. This part of the process is never a one way street.

Reaching out also involves trust. You must be willing to be open and honest with those who are walking the same journey with you. If there is not trust, there will not be honest communication. The moment you start playing a game with this person, they will walk away.

Trust is really about what you feel about yourself. If your self worth is high, you will be willing to be open with those who are in your life to challenge your design and offer you greater clarity. Without trust your skepticism will push them away. They will leave and you will lose the purpose of their pausing in your life.

I am a strong believer in angels being around your life. I have had too many experiences where a person has entered my life for a moment. Yet, in that moment their pausing has brought clarity and growth to my life. When their mission was fulfilled, they moved on.

For years my life was a series of situations. Each situation just brought more clutter to my life. Why? The clutter was not about breaking free from the Circle of Sameness. It was behavior designed to hold me a hostage to my yesterday. I was a prisoner serving a self imposed sentence.

Only when I learned the process was I able to turn situations into lessons and remove the clutter through creating experiences designed to make me better, smarter and taller.

You see, a situation is an event in your life where no lesson is learned. That situation gets filtered through negative emotions and filed in an open file. When you are faced with a difficulty, these are the files you go to for understanding. Without the lesson there is nothing to get you beyond it. The new situation is stacked on top of the old situation and you create clutter. Clutter is anything you start, but don't finish.

An experience is an event in your life where you learn the lesson. The filtering process is different. It gets filled with positive energy and filed in a mental file designed to free you from the Circle of Sameness. With the lesson comes understanding; with the understanding comes calmness; with the calmness comes clarity; with the clarity comes the confidence; with the confidence comes the freedom; with the freedom comes an unlimited today.

The process is simple to read, but challenging to implement. You must:

- *Face what is really happening in your life.*

- *Redesign the behaviors that have made it okay.*

- *Strengthen the good things about you.*

- *Reach out to others who are there to make you better.*

Notes

Chapter 5
THE LESSONS

Life is about the lessons there are for people to learn.
Without the lessons a person will lack the
understanding necessary to continue to move
their life forward.

I am proud of my life! I'm proud of who I am and what I have achieved. That hasn't always been true. I lived for years wrestling with why *God saw fit to let me be brought into this world.* I wrestled for years with why a mother who conceived me didn't want me. I struggled with why someone would adopt me and then, just throw me away like you would a piece of clothing you had outgrown. I struggled for years striving to understand why my dad could tell me *I love you* and then drive off and leave me standing on a corner in the darkest moment of my life.

My life was an emotional roller coaster. I was up and then I was down. The "New Me" would experience a moment of growth and that would cause the "Old Me" to get angry and attack with a vicious fury. Because the "Old Me" was stronger, the "New Me" would get shoved back into the closet and I would start the down cycle all over again.

That kept me frustrated; and that fed the "Old Me." I just kept playing the old negative tapes, and that continued to feed the "Old Me." All that achieved was to make today a repeat of yesterday, and that strengthened the "Old Me." The stronger the "Old Me" got the harder it was to break out of my Circle of Sameness.

That Circle of Sameness kept me a prisoner in my own life. That Circle of Sameness wouldn't let me see any other possibilities. That Circle of Sameness was a never ending track that kept stealing my positive beliefs and creating a belief system that said *this is your life!* The stronger that self limiting belief, the more challenging it was to exit the Circle of Sameness.

The exit door was always there; I just wasn't emotionally prepared to see it. The exit door was never hidden; I was so caught up in playing my negative tapes that I couldn't find it. The exit door was always visible, but my negative journey kept me staring at the circle rather than really searching for the exit.

It was when I discovered the process, that my mental sight became stronger than my emotional drive. Only when I was able to implement the process, was I able to break out of the Circle of Sameness.
Only when I learned to:
- *Face what was really happening in my life*
- *Redesign the journey I was taking*
- *Strengthen my talents*
- *Reach out to those who could make me better*

did I break free of all the negative tapes the "Old Me"

was using to keep me a prisoner in my yesterday. Only when I became strong enough to stay focused on the "New Me" could I challenge the "Old Me" with the confidence that I could win the battle for the emotional control of my life.

This journey to allowing the "New Me" to have control over my life is not over. As far as I have come, those old negative tapes are still filed in a filing cabinet in my mind. The "Old Me" is not dead; he is just put away. BUT — if I don't stay focused on my personal improvement, he can come back. That means *I must continue to make the process a daily part of my life.* That means *I must manage the pace of my life.* If that pace is moving faster than my mental clarity, I free the "Old Me" to once again rule my life. With that comes the freedom for the "Old Me" to raise his ugly head and emotionally beat the "New Me" back into the dark closet where all the old tapes stand guard over the exit.

Lessons are the foundation on which you build your life.

To keep this from happening I must constantly revisit the lessons I have learned from my journey. These lessons have created the pages of my personal growth journal. Their power goes beyond the yesterday where they were learned; these lessons stretch into today and are a key to tomorrow. These lessons form the foundation on which I continue to build my life.

Lesson #1: I have choices!

What an important lesson this was for me to learn. Before I gained this realization, I didn't understand *I didn't have to do what others told me I had to do!* I had the right to make a choice; I had the right to decide for myself.

Granted, at first I took it to the extreme. When I first started this journey, my choices were about rebelling, not improving. At first it was *my way or the highway.* It took time and maturity to understand the responsibility that goes with the right to make choices.

One major thing I learned was *in a crisis you don't make decisions. You only implement a thought designed to get you through that moment.* After the moment is over the event still remains.

For several years I was challenged by the fact that I would work through issues, feel good for the moment and then find the same issue reappearing in my life. My heart would sink when I found myself facing what I thought I had completed. There was also a sense of anger that came with this realization. *Why wouldn't this go away! I had been here before and had dealt with this.*

The realization was *Yes, I had been there before, but the environment in which I was dealing with the event was not designed for decision making.* It was designed to just get me through that moment. The environment was something the "Old Me" used to fool me into thinking I was dealing with the situation.

The choice I had made was a reaction, not a response. Without realizing it, I was simply designing a process to have to keep repeating the same event over and over. I soon learned *if I wanted to get beyond events, I had to calm down in order to have the clarity necessary to face the issue.* What freedom there was when I realized I wasn't making choices. I was being fooled by the "Old Me."

Now, as an event would happen, I would step back and ask myself three questions:
- *What is happening here?*
- *What do I need to do to face this issue?*
- *What is the lesson contained in this challenge?*

Each question was designed to slow me down. The slower I moved emotionally, the calmer I became. The calmer I became the more clarity my mind had. The greater the clarity, the more I was able to understand what was happening.

In working with people I have learned that when a situation hits a life the tendency is to speed up and try to race through it. That simply feeds the "Old Self."

The "Old Self" loves it when you speed up. The faster you move the less control you have. Any choice you make will not lead you to a solution; it will simply be about "getting through this." That will guarantee you will face this event again and again.

The lesson is <u>every time you feel you need to speed up it is a sign that you need to slow down.</u> Getting beyond means finding a solution that gives you a lesson, rather than racing through and creating a momentary escape.

You have the right to choose what you do with any event in your life. Just make sure what you are doing is choosing a solution, not continuing to travel the Circle of Sameness.

There is freedom in knowing *I have the right to make choices!*

Lesson #2: Why Spend My Energy Being A Carbon Copy When I Am The Original!

This has become another point of freedom in my life. Not only can I make choices, but I can choose to be me. To achieve that I must know who I am.

I have worked with many people who spend each day as an actor in someone else's play, simply because they don't know who they are. That simple fact forces them to be a carbon copy. With that behavior they will not find happiness, personal fulfillment or freedom. They will constantly depend on others to tell them who they are, what they can achieve and where they can go. These people will become a groupie with anyone who is willing to plan their life for them.

If you stop and look at this, isn't it a sad thought? Each person is an individual, but few ever live their life as the individual they were designed to be. Each person is created to live their dream, but few ever get to color their own life. Each person is free to be what their talents will allow them to be, but few ever take their talents to the level that grants them their individuality.

I understand this! For years I was afraid to search for who I was. For years I hid behind what others told me I could do.

My relationship with God is such an important part of my life. My relationship with Him has gotten me through the tough times. If there is one thing I have learned, I can depend on Him.

When I was growing up, my mother always sent my sisters and me to church. My parents never went, but my sisters and I were there for every church function. I liked church; it was time out of the house and it just felt good.

I have always had the knack for speaking in front of people. It has been something that comes naturally to me. In Sunday School I was always the one called on to do things in front of the group. Several times people asked me *have you ever thought of being a preacher?* It had never really crossed my mind, but when you are asked the same question over and over, you begin to think *that is what I'm supposed to be.*

After college I headed for Seminary. There was always a gnawing feeling inside me that questioned what I was doing. BUT, people thought I would be a good preacher, and I didn't have any other plan.

I finished Seminary and had several churches talk to me about becoming their Pastor. There was something missing each time I would consider being the Pastor of a church. BUT, there was this nagging voice that kept asking *what is wrong with you? This is what others told you that you should be doing.* There was guilt; there was doubt; there was fear; there were all these emotions that kept hounding me.

It was Billy Barber, the Pastor of First Baptist Church in Tampa, that helped me realize *I didn't have to be what others said I had to be.* I was not only free to make my own choice, but to be an original. Armed with the assurance that I could be whatever I wanted to be, I found myself in the classroom challenging the minds of students. There I felt joy and a sense of personal fulfillment.

There was so much freedom in being the original I was created to be. It is tragic how many people never learn this lesson. They spend their time on this earth being what they have been programed to be, rather than being the original they were created to become. They get up each day and exist in a world that doesn't give them freedom. It is the world where the Circle of Sameness holds them hostage.

I find it amazing how many times I asked those in my audience *if you were not afraid, would you be doing anything differently with your life?* You can see the looks on their faces; you can feel the emotional answer to the question. Yet, the "Old Self" has them so programed with fear that they can't see beyond the limitation they have settled for.

Lesson #3: I have a mind to use!

This was another challenge for me. For years my mother told me *you are the stupidest kid I have ever known.* What do you think happens when one of the two most important people in your life keeps beating you down with those words? Yes, I believed it! I thought I was a real dummy. Oh, I made good grades. BUT, according to my mother, *good grades don't mean you are smart.*

For as long as I can remember I have had a very active mind. It has always been a part of me that wouldn't turn off. I used to write poetry and throw it away. After all, if you are not smart, you can't write. I would write short stories and throw them away. Again, if you are not smart, you can't write.

It was my debate coach in high school who really pushed me. I had taken several speech classes from Mr.

Brown. After every speech he would help me develop my presentation skills. He entered me in speech tournaments and I would win! Mr. Brown constantly told me how intelligent I was. He would marvel at the creative speeches I would write. He believed in me and wouldn't let me put myself down.

After I left home he stepped up his presence in my life and got me involved in debate. During my senior year in high school my partner and I made it to the national debate finals. We lost, but that experience was an important part of my development.

I love my mind! Does that sound strange? I play in my imagination all the time. I love taking an idea and exploring it. I love creating thoughts and pushing them to the limits. I have a creative mind, and I don't want to waste it.

Too many people don't think; they think they think, but they don't think. They don't use the creativeness that is within every human. Your mind is only limited by you! When you stop playing in your imagination, you turn your creative nature off! When your imagination is turned off, you tend to look at, talk about and relive yesterday. Any time I meet a person who spends their energy talking about the "good old days," I know I have met a person who has lost their creative juices.

The mind is not about reliving yesterday. The mind is about taking the journey you have been on and creating a today filled with lessons and information that will allow tomorrow to be even better.

The more you turn your imagination loose, the more creative you become. The more you look at today as your living room of experiences, the more possibilities you allow your mind to see.

Don't forget it! *Those who live in yesterday are trapped in the Circle of Sameness.* That Circle of Sameness is controlled by the "Old You." The "Old You" doesn't want you to use your mind. The "Old You" knows that the more you develop your mind the less control the "Old You" will have over your life. So, when you go through those times when your imagination is free to play, the "Old You" will raise its ugly head and take you through all the negative emotions it can muster.

The reality is, *you have a mind that is highly creative. Don't waste it!*

Lesson #4: I am a brand name!

Someone once said *God didn't create any junk!* Know what? They were correct!

Years ago if you had heard me talk about myself, you would have heard me doing two things:

- *Putting myself down.*

- *Asking you to tell me I was okay.*

113

Neither of these was designed to build my self worth. In fact every time I put myself down I fed the negative tapes the "Old Me" was using to hold me hostage.

People used to talk to me about self image. I didn't understand what they were saying. Only when I really started my personal growth journey did I begin to understand the concept of "self." The real issue is not self image; the real issue is self worth.

The real issue is self worth, not self esteem.

I believe it works like this:

self worth ■> self esteem ■> self image ■> self confidence

The foundation I must build on is my self worth. It is from this that all the rest of my feelings about me spring. Know what I learned? *It was on the ledge at the hotel that I learned what I felt about me.*

I remember being sixteen and checking into the hotel, going to the seventh floor, putting the key in the door, opening the door, dropping the suitcase, walking across the room, opening the window, and sitting on that ledge for five hours. There were so many things going through my mind.

- *How could they do this to me? I must be a terrible person.*

- *What is wrong with me that even my parents don't want me?*

- *There really isn't anything to live for.*

Yet, there was something inside me that wouldn't let me jump. There was something inside me that kept screaming *if you jump, your mother will win. Don't give her that victory.*

Without knowing it, my self worth was at work. It wouldn't let me give in to all the negative messages I had been programed with by my mother. It wouldn't let me give up. There was a reason to live; there was a reason to get out of bed tomorrow; there was a purpose to my life.

I remember crawling back into the room, looking in the mirror and saying to myself *I want to live.* That belief has never left me. It has taken me through the dark valleys; it has guided me through those moments when I questioned my life; it has calmed me in the midst of uncertain terrain. It has helped me to see myself as a Brand Name!

Every day you express your self worth through your behavior. If you want to learn about a person, study their behavior. Words are simply an instrument we use to convey our thoughts. Behavior is the design that explains what you feel about yourself.

When you don't see yourself as a Brand Name, your allow the "Old You" to control you with the old negative tapes. These tapes attach themselves to negative emotions which trigger negative impressions in your mind and express themselves through negative feelings. Tie all these together and you act out these feelings in the form of negative behavior.

When you believe you are a Brand Name, a person of worth, you will fight the "Old You" as it works to turn on the old negative tapes. You won't allow the "Old You" to rule your life with old negative tapes. You know you are beyond that. You know you are a Brand Name!

Recently, I was talking with Drew in one of our sessions. We had been working together for ten months. Each of my Private Coaching students has a study guide I design for them. One part of their Growth Journal is a monthly recap of the major frustrations they have felt in the four rooms of their life. For several months Drew's frustration sheet had been filled. But for the last couple of months he had been challenged to find any major frustrations.

We sat, stared at the sheet and just grinned. We knew what was happening. He was now strong enough to recognize the tactics of the "Old You." He was now strong enough to face that "Old Person" and not allow him to rule his life.

Hey, as you free yourself from that "Old Person" who rules your life from the negative side, you cease to have as many frustrations. As the frustrations diminish, your inner calmness takes over. As the inner calmness takes over you gain clarity. The greater your clarity the less control the "Old You" has over your life. As the "New You" takes control, your picture of you begins to be redrawn. One of the crayons you use to redraw your life is self worth. The stronger the self worth the greater your personal value. You really are a Brand Name!

Lesson #5: I am a spiritual person!

This is so important to me. It is a central part of my personal growth journey. I sincerely believe I have a spiritual guide. There have been too many positives for me to believe they were just an accident.

My faith in God is the inner strength I draw from. There are still times when certain things happen and the old tapes flip on. As strong as you may become, you will never completely get beyond the ability of the "Old You" to throw emotional darts at your life. As strong as your spiritual faith may be, there will be moments when it is tested by events in your life. It is in these moments you will know the importance of being a spiritual person.

When those moments of uncertainty happen, I need the inner strength to get me through. When those times occur, I reach inside and draw from my spiritual strength.

I have had people say to me *that is just another emotional crutch.* They can call it what they want, but I know it goes beyond the need for an emotional crutch. I know there is a spiritual guide, I know there is a God who directs my life. The more I seek His guidance the calmer my life becomes. The more I seek His will for my life the clearer my journey becomes. The more I trust Him as the Guide for my life the sharper I become as a person.

I am a spiritual person!

Lesson #6: I am alone!

This lesson has been very important for me to learn. It is the lesson of personal responsibility. It is the process that wouldn't allow me to blame others for my life.

For years I blamed my mother for everything that was wrong with me. Then, I realized I had a choice! What I did with my yesterday was up to me. I could let it emotionally own me and suck the life out of me, or I could choose to take where I had been and use it as my personal growth center. I chose to take my yesterday, find the lessons and use it to improve me as a person. In doing that I had to face myself.

That meant I had to take responsibility for the decisions I made. It meant I had to hold myself accountable for my behavior. When I stopped looking for someone or something to blame, I began to understand living from the inside-out.

For years I had lived from the outside in. I would get up each day and look for what I could find to blame for what was either wrong or not happening in my life. When I found that "something," I could justify my behavior. That meant I never had to be responsible or accountable for my behavior. The interesting thing was that many around my life let me do just that. Hey, if they were validating my behavior, it must be okay.

In the design that uses blame there is no growth. In blame there are only reasons and excuses. As long as that is your behavior, you are trapped in the Circle of Sameness. You have designed your life to kill your inner spirit and accept what is as what will always be. In reality you have given up on improving. It becomes what you talk about, not what is happening.

It was Spencer Hayes who hit me between the eyes with the question *when are you going to stop blaming others, take responsibility for who you are and get on with your life?* That really made me angry. Who did he think he was to ask me that! Didn't he understand what I had been through! Why, what had happened to me as a child was cruel; it was wrong; it should not have been done.

Yes, my childhood was cruel! Yes, it was wrong! Yes, it should not have been done! All those things were true, but how long was I going to hang onto them as the reason I wasn't getting beyond yesterday's negatives? Spencer was right. I needed to get beyond all those yesterday tapes and get on with my life.

I needed to face the fact that my yesterday happened, but I had a choice of what to do with it. My yesterday could destroy me or make me a better person. Those were my only two options.

If I chose to let it destroy me, then I would spend the rest of my life as a person who sought every excuse in the world for living my life less fully than it was intended to be lived. I had that choice. BUT, with that choice came a journey. Was that the journey I wanted for my life? Did I want to live my life looking outwardly for reasons and excuses to justify what I was not doing? NO!!!!!!

Then, I was left with only one choice. I had to use my yesterday as a source of strength. I had to take my yesterday and learn from where I had been. I had to find what was good in all that appeared so bad.

That was a different mind set. That demanded a different framework of thought. I had to go inside and rewrite the scripts. I had to take responsibility for my today and stop blaming my yesterday. As long as I blamed today on yesterday, all I did was repeat all the old negative tapes. That gave the "Old Me" total control of my life.

This was a challenging time for me. It was a struggle to get beyond the behaviors I had accepted as okay. It was challenging to rewrite the scripts. To do that I had to go inside myself. I had let go of all my outside ways and go inside myself and face me. I was alone. There was no longer anyone to blame. I had to face me and decide what I wanted for my life.

I am not sure people understand that with each event you create a script. It is from that script you find the meaning of the event. Most people don't face the real issues, therefore the script they write is filled with negative story lines. Each time you reread the script you enhance the negative story lines and make the pain larger. Over a period of time you forget all the other things that go with the story. The pain, the negatives, become the story, rather than one part of the story.

I took my yesterday apart and worked through the story. I wouldn't stop until I could find a lesson I could use to improve myself. I wouldn't wish my yesterday on anyone, nor would I change it. The greatest lesson I came away with was *if it had never happened to me, I wouldn't be who I am today.*

That is so important. It taught me to look at life from the inside out. It taught me that in every perceived negative there is a positive. The positive doesn't always jump out at you. If you arc looking for a justification or a reason, you will feed on the negative. There are always others who are doing the same and will support your effort. That means you are using the outer part of your life to justify your behavior.

You don't learn because you go through an event; you learn when your life is tested.

When you position yourself to live life to the fullest, you accept what your life has been handed. You know that in every event there is a lesson that will make you a better person. That lesson doesn't always jump out at you. You have to slow down, face the event and find it. Once you find it, you will then be tested to see if you have really learned it. You don't learn because you go through something; you learn when you pass the test.

I tell people daily *you won't learn anything in my seminar. All you will do is gather information. Once you leave this room, you will be tested on the information you have gathered. It is at that point you will know whether you learned anything.*

If you repeat your same old pattern of behavior, you didn't learn. You simply spent some time gathering more information to store in your junk file. If you face the event and bring new behavior, you have learned and will move beyond that event's ability to hold you hostage.

Others can't apply the information you have

gathered for you. At this point you are alone. It is your decision. If someone else does it for you, you are an actor in their thought processes. It must be your choice; it must be you implementing it; it must be you taking responsibility for your life. You are alone. You are perfectly designed to achieve what you are achieving. It is your life; your choices; your design; your journey!

You are Alone!

Lesson #7: I must have a dream!

I was like a lot of people. I would write goals and then get frustrated when I didn't reach them. I thought simply having goals was what was important. It took time, but I soon learned *writing goals without a dream to connect them to is a fantasy.*

I was setting myself up to have to repeat yesterday. Without a connection point for my goals I had nothing to create different actions. So, in that design I could only repeat yesterday. I would play all the old negative tapes and become frustrated because nothing new was happening in my life.

There was something missing. That something was a dream for my life. I needed a mental picture that focused me on tomorrow, rather than yesterday. I needed a mental picture to give today a purpose in my life. Without that dream today was simply time and space. I would get up, do my "to do" list and then wander throughout the day. I would fill it with action, but that action was about surviving the day not improving my life. At the end of the day I would be exhausted, frustrated and feeling as though I hadn't achieved anything. Know what? Those feelings were correct. I had simply existed and survived another day. I have strengthened the "Old Me" and denied the "New Me" the opportunity for improvement. This design made me a hostage in my own life.

I needed that "something" to free me from yesterday. I needed that "something" to make my today a growth experience, not a repeat. That something was a dream for my life.

I would not have been able to achieve this if I had not learned the lesson of living from the Inside Out. When you live your life based on looking outward, you understand life based on what you see happening. Your definitions are drawn from a lack of internal understanding.

When you live your life from the Inside Out, you draw from your inner desires and thoughts. You have a sketch in your imagination you are coloring each day with your behavior. You understand based on the sketch in your imagination, not the blank screen that comes from living from the Outside In.

To find my dream I had to slow down and ask myself three questions. They had to come in one order;

I couldn't go forward until I had answered the question that was in front of me.

1. What Do I Really Want For My Life?

2. Why Do I Really Want This For My Life?

3. What Price Am I Willing To Pay To Achieve It?

With the first question, ***What Do I Really Want For My Life?,*** I could establish a direction for my life. Without a direction each day was a crap shoot. I would get up and "hope" something good would happen. If it didn't, I had just wasted another day of my life. What I didn't understand was *even if the good happened, I wasn't prepared to see it.* Therefore, it was happening, but because I had no connection point for the action I was taking, I missed it.

Once I had a direction, I could see the meaning for what was going on around me. That direction gave me a different sight; that direction slowed me down; that direction gave me that connection point between the action and my mind.

With the second question, ***Why Do I Really Want This For My Life?,*** I could find my true motivation. There are only three things that can motivate a human:

* *Knowing that they matter*
* *Being part of a crusade*
* *Living their dream.*

The challenge with the first two is they are outside driven. They are based on an external creating the motivation. As long as you know you matter, there is motivation. What happens if you don't feel you matter? The motivation goes away.

As long as there is a crusade, you are motivated. What happens if the crusade ends? You have to find another crusade to feed this motivation.

The dream is not outside motivation. It is inside driven. It is your mind sketching possibilities; it is your emotions creating the energy to turn the sketch into action. It is you gathering the calmness, clarity and confidence to push forward, rather than repeating where you have already been.

Your motivation is controlled by the sketch in your imagination. Your imagination, which is the nerve center for tomorrow, is actively coloring the picture with possibilities. It is strengthening your mind with resilience. It is you believing in the possibility of tomorrow. That makes today very exciting.

With the third question, *What Price Am I Willing To Pay To Achieve It?,* I know how far I am willing to go. Life doesn't break down because of a lack of desire; life comes apart at the price tag. I have watched hundreds walk away from their stated dream, not because they didn't desire to have it, but because the mental, emotional, physical or financial price tag was more than they were willing to pay.

It is here that the rubber meets the road. It is here where you are really tested. It is here where the real decisions are made. "Too tough" really means *the price is more than I am willing to pay.* When the price tag is too great, the sketch loses it color. When the price tag is too great, the energy needed to feed its forward movement stops. When the price tag is too great the calmness, clarity and confidence are replaced with worry, doubt and uncertainty. At that point the "Old You" takes over the journey. At that point there is no new tomorrow; there is only a repeat of yesterday. At that point the dream turns to a wish that you hope someday you can achieve.

To move forward, to create a better tomorrow, to free myself from the chains of yesterday, I must have a dream. I must have that sketch in my imagination that gives tomorrow color and today purpose. I must have a dream.

The great challenge for all of us is to overcome the power the "Old You" has over our life. As long as the "Old You" is in control, the negative tapes will continue to turn on and emotionally pull us down. As long as that is happening in your life, you will be trapped in the Circle of Sameness.

To break free you must:

- *Face what is happening in your life.*

- *Redesign what is allowing the old tapes to turn on.*

- *Strengthen those things that you are good at doing.*

- *Reach out to others who can help you complete your journey.*

The reality is: *you will either get beyond yesterday's tapes or they will continue to rule your life and cause you to miss what your life can really be.*

It is your choice.

Remember,

You are perfectly designed to achieve what you are achieving.

Programs by Richard Flint, CSP

Leadership/Management
A Day At The Zoo
Building A Partnership With Your People
Leadership & Profitability
No Excuse Management
Retaining & Recruiting Quality People
The Promise of Leadership
Understanding Motivation

Sales Training
As Professional As You Can Be!
Developing An Effective Sales Presentation
No Limits!
The Art of Bringing The Customer Back
Strengthening The Total Sales Process Series

Customer Care
Beyond Service, The Personal Touch
Strengthening The Customer Relationship
The Art of Bringing The Customer Back

Personal Motivation
Achieving Balance In Your Life
Controlling The Stress In Your Life
Do You Have What It Takes?
Do You Really Want It?
It's All About Being Better
It's Time To Do Something With Your Life!
Join The Celebration!
No Limits!

Spouse/Family
Achieving Balance In Your Life
If Marriages Are Made In Heaven, Why Can't They Be Endured On Earth?
Living In The Four Room Stress House
Strengthening The Family

For More Information:

Visit us on the web!

www.RichardFlint.com

Richard Flint Seminars
11835 Canon Blvd., Suite C-105, Newport News, VA, 23606
1-800-368-8255 or (757) 873-7722

Notes